新世纪普通高等教育经济与贸易类课程规划教材

外贸函电
WAIMAO HANDIAN

主　编　刘　卉
副主编　陈曦明　马瑞雪
编　者　寇金南　蒋立真

大连理工大学出版社

图书在版编目(CIP)数据

外贸函电 / 刘卉主编． -- 大连：大连理工大学出版社，2024.1（2024.1重印）
新世纪普通高等教育经济与贸易类课程规划教材
ISBN 978-7-5685-4106-0

Ⅰ．①外… Ⅱ．①刘… Ⅲ．①对外贸易－英语－电报信函－高等学校－教材 Ⅳ．①F75

中国国家版本馆CIP数据核字（2023）第003561号

大连理工大学出版社出版
地址：大连市软件园路80号　　邮政编码：116023
发行：0411-84708842　邮购：0411-84708973　传真：0411-84701466
E-mail：dutp@dutp.cn　　URL：https://www.dutp.cn
辽宁虎驰科技传媒有限公司印刷　　大连理工大学出版社发行

幅面尺寸：185mm×260mm	印张：17.25	字数：320千字
2024年1月第1版		2024年1月第2次印刷

责任编辑：苏绘泉　　　　　　　　　　　责任校对：鞠　欣
封面设计：张　莹

ISBN 978-7-5685-4106-0　　　　　　　　　　　定价：48.00元

本书如有印装质量问题，请与我社发行部联系更换。

PREFACE 前言

一、教材定位

"外贸函电"是国际贸易的重要内容,是国际贸易专业、商务英语专业的必修课程。"外贸函电"将对外贸易业务与英语融为一体,主要讲授对外贸易业务各个环节的知识,同时培养学生在相关业务环节的英语表达能力。本教材旨在培养新文科的复合型人才,引导学生系统学习外贸业务,了解并熟悉进出口的关键步骤,重点掌握外贸业务信函的撰写要求,在内容学习过程中进一步夯实英语书写能力,向高级商务英语进阶。

二、教材特色

本教材可供商务英语、国际贸易、工商管理学专业本科第5~7学期开设的国际商务谈判、商务英语写作、国际贸易函电等课程使用。

本教材本着"理解先行,实践导向"的原则,从概念入手,引导学生了解国际贸易的基本概念和重点表达,在全面、准确理解概念的基础上,进行模仿、分析、评价、创造等学习过程。本教材包括建立客户业务关系、询价、报盘、还盘、订货、接受、签约、包装、装运、交付、结算、保险、商检、索赔、代理及仲裁等贸易步骤,通过写作实例帮助学生快速掌握外贸电函的框架和具体内容。

本教材利用大连理工大学多年成熟的教学经验和技术支持,基于"成果导向"的教育理念,重点参考互联网的传播特点,结合新时代中国特色社会主义思想的学习,设计了"学习目标""学习任务""学习重点""自我测评"4个栏目的教学活动。

三、教学资源

教学资源是保障教材有效使用的必要支撑。本教材提供各单元的练习答案，同时配套电子课件和微课视频，供教师备课参考和学生课外学习使用。

本教材由大连理工大学教师团队编写而成，主编刘卉老师负责第2~8章、第11~12章的编写，及统筹审校工作；寇金南老师负责第1章的编写，马瑞雪老师负责第9~10章的编写，陈曦明老师负责第13~15章的编写；蒋立真老师负责全书的审校工作。

在编写本教材的过程中，编者参考、引用和改编了国内外出版物中的相关资料以及网络资源，在此表示深深的谢意！相关著作权人看到本教材后，请与出版社联系，出版社将按照相关法律的规定支付稿酬。

尽管我们在教材建设的特色方面做出了许多努力，但由于编者水平有限，书中不足之处在所难免，恳请各教学单位、教师及广大读者批评指正。

编　者

2024 年 1 月

所有意见和建议请发往：dutpbk@163.com

欢迎访问高教数字化服务平台：https://www.dutp.cn/hep/

联系电话：0411-84708445　84708462

CONTENTS

Unit One　Basic Knowledge of Business Correspondences ·············· 1

Unit Two　Effective Business Writing ·············· 19

Unit Three　Enquiry ·············· 39

Unit Four　Replies and Quotation ·············· 53

Unit Five　Counter-offer ·············· 69

Unit Six　Order ·············· 85

Unit Seven　Payment ·············· 103

Unit Eight　Requests for Payment & Replies ·············· 125

Unit Nine　Transportation ·············· 143

Unit Ten　Insurance ·············· 157

Unit Eleven　Complaints & Claims ·············· 171

Unit Twelve　Adjustments ·············· 187

Unit Thirteen　Agent & Agency ·············· 203

Unit Fourteen　Good, Neutral & Bad Messages ·············· 223

Unit Fifteen　Miscellaneous Correspondence ·············· 247

Unit One
Basic Knowledge of Business Correspondences

Business writing has been around as long as business and writing. Thousands of years ago business people kept track of transactions and inventory through writing. As more international business became usual, business letters became a huge aspect of the business world. In the professional world, you will often need to write a business letter. From applying for a new job, writing a thank-you note, sending a note of apology or a farewell email when you depart, there are many circumstances where an appropriately formatled letter is required

Unit Objectives

After learning this unit, students should be able to:
1. Understand the definition and functions of business letters;
2. Grasp the structure of traditional business letters, faxes and emails;
3. Apply the basic principles of business letter writing into practice.

Definition and Functions of Business Letters

A business letter is a formal document with a set structure, often sent from one company to another or from a company to its clients, employees, and stakeholders. Business letters are used for professional correspondence between individuals, as well. In general, the purpose of business writing is to communicate with other business people through the means of writing.

The different types of business writing will communicate information differently to the recipient. There are several main categories of business writing. First, there is email. This is the least formal communication method, and is generally used when people are not able to physically get up and talk to someone, or to communicate without the use of a phone. Research and technical writing are used in the business world to create presentations and document new ideas for companies.

Although email has taken over as the most common form of correspondence, traditional business letters (TBL) and faxes are still used for many important, serious types of correspondence, including reference letters, employment verification, job offers, and more. A business letter or fax is a more formal way of communicating information to a colleague or superior. Business letters are often used when applying for a job. Faxes are also often used to send important information to groups of people.

Structure of Business Letters

Writing an effective, polished business letter can be an easy task, so long as you adhere to the established rules for layout and language. Make the purpose of your letter clear through simple and targeted language, and keep the opening paragraph brief. You can start with, "I am writing in reference to…" and from there, communicate only what you need to say. The subsequent paragraphs should include information that gives your reader(s) a full understanding of your objective(s) but avoid meandering sentences and needlessly long words. Each section of your letter should adhere to the appropriate format, start with your contact information and that of your recipient's, salutation, the body of the letter, closing, and finally, your signature.

❖ Your Contact Information

Your Name
Your Job Title
Your Company
Your Address
City, State Zip Code
Your Phone Number
Your Email Address

❖ The Date

The date you're penning the correspondence

❖ Recipient's Contact Information

Their Name
Their Title
Their Company
The Company's Address
City, State Zip Code

❖ The Salutation

Use "To Whom It May Concern," if you're unsure specifically whom you're addressing.

Use the formal salutation "Dear Mr./Ms./Dr. [Last Name]," if you know the recipient.

Use "Dear [First Name]," only if you have an informal relationship with the recipient.

❖ The Body

Use single-spaced lines with an added space between each paragraph, after the salutation, and above the closing.

Left justify your letter (against the left margin).

❖ Closing Salutation

Keep your closing paragraph to two sentences. Simply reiterate your reason for writing and thank the reader for considering your request. Some good options for your closing include:

Respectfully yours
Yours sincerely
Cordially
Respectfully

If your letter is **less formal**, consider using:
All the best
Best
Thank you
Regards

❖ Your Signature

Write your signature just beneath your closing and leave four single spaces between your closing and your typed full name, title, phone number, email address, and any other contact information you want to include. Use the format as follows:

Your handwritten signature
Typed full name
Title

If you're sending an email letter, your signature will be slightly different. Rather than including your contact information in the heading of the letter, list it below your signature. For example:

Yours sincerely,
First Name Last Name
Title
Your Address
Your Phone Number
Your Email Address

Layout of a Traditional Business Letter

As you can see from the example below, a business letter has a very defined format. Writing a good business letter is all about understanding the formatting conventions employed in each element of the letter itself. The letter below is from a university to a company. It shows the basic features of a traditional business letter.

Example One

Jane Lee University of Technology No.2 Technology Street, Dalian Liaoning, PRC 116023 86-411-5555555 Jane@email.com	Sender's address
March 15, 2021	Date
	Inside address
John Wong Managing Editor	

Acme Graphic & Design 123 Business Rd. Beijing, PRC 100000 Dear Mr. Wong,	Salutation
I would like to invite you to attend our upcoming Liberal Arts Department job networking event. The event will be held on the afternoon of May 1, 2022. We wish to provide our graduating seniors with an opportunity to meet business leaders in the area who may be looking for new hires who hold degrees in the Liberal Arts. The event will be held at the Student Center at University of Technology and will last about two to three hours. If you have an interest in attending or sending a company representative to meet with our students, please let me know at your earliest convenience and I can reserve a table for you. Thanks for your time and I hope to hear from you soon.	Body of the letter
Respectfully, (signature hard copy letter)	Complimentary close
Jane Lee Liberal Arts Department Chair	Signature

Layout of a Business Email

Emails are short letters for various purposes. They can be used to quickly, efficiently and effectively communicate with a large audience or to convey an idea to a single person. Nowadays, most small businesses use personal email for professional use. Clear, effective communication begins with using the proper business email format. An email usually consists of the following parts: the sender's email address, the recipient's email address, the subject and the body, the complimentary close and the name of the sender. The emails below show the basic features of a business email.

Example Two

To: Ms. Lindsay Wells@hotmail.com cc: David Nash bcc: Kenny Turner From: Nathan Chen@yeah.net Subject: Order Received	Header information
Dear Ms. Wells: Thank you for your order for 20 units of our porcelain pillows. Your order has been given priority and we will keep you informed of its development. Thank you for your patronage.	Message text
Nathan Chen Handan Pottery	Signature

Example Three

To: Mr. Oscar Bell From: Zhipinig Liang cc: Paul Josh Subject: attending sports meeting	Email head
Dear Mr. Oscar Bell: You are warmly invited to be the guest of our postgraduates' sports meeting, hosted by the Graduate's Union in the school stadium and held at 1:30 pm on May 26th. The purpose of this meeting is to celebrate the 60th anniversary of the founding of Dalian University of Technology. We hope you will be able to accept this invitation. And we would appreciate it if you could inform us of your decision beforehand.	Body
Yours, Zhiping Liang	Signature

Layout of a Business Fax

A fax is a widely used means for telecommunication in business especially when speed is important and the recipient does not have email. The contents can be handwritten or typed according to the formality required. A fax consists of three parts:

1. The person who sends and the person who receives the fax, their positions, addresses, the organizations the sender and the receiver work for, date, and subject;
2. The fax number, pages of the fax;
3. The subject, the brief generalization of the content of the fax, so that its content can be generally known by the receiver before the main part is read. The subject takes the form of phrases rather than sentences.

The format of the second and third parts is the same as that of letters. It is often the case that companies have paper specially used for faxes, with the address of the company, telephone number, and fax number printed on it. In writing the body of fax message, you can follow the common practices for writing business letters, but the salutation and complimentary close are generally omitted. However, there is usually a signature in the end. The fax below shows the basic features of a business fax.

Example Four

FAX TRANSMISSION	ELECTROLUBE
	A division of HK Wentworth Ltd
	Wentworth House
	Blakes Road, Wargrave
	Berkshire, RG10 8AW
	England
	Tel: +44 0734 404031
	Fax: +44 0734 403084

Fax head

TO: Sarah Morton From: Helen Thompson
COMPANY: Anoing Electronic Components Ltd Date: 6 June, 2019
Fax No: 010 6334047 PAGES INC THIS SHEET: 1
SUBJECT: LEADTIMES

Receiver's & sender's fax head

I am pleased to confirm that the following products are still available:

Fax body

PCC 400H, AFC400H, SBU000, CPL200H, EAD400HFRE400H Regards, Helen Thompson UK Order Processing	Signature

Example Five

Fax Message		Fax heading
To: Mr. Larry Lyon From: Jack Kingsbury Fax No. : (0214) 7612002 Fax No: (0411)8775639 Date: March 15, 2021 Page (s) : 1 Subject: REPLACEMENTS		
Please airfreight 3 overhead projectors to replace the ones damaged in transit, as they are urgently needed for the meeting to be held next Monday.		Message
Jack Kingsbury		Signature

Principles of Writing Business Correspondences

Writing an effective business letter is an important skill no matter what type of job you hold. Although business communications have become much more casual with the advent of the Internet and email, there are still times when a formal letter is required. Understanding the principles of business letter writing can help you ensure that your letter is clear and concise.

❖ Be Neat and Clean

Business letters should be neat and error-free. A business letter represents both you and your employer, so whether the letter comes from you or your administrative staff, it should look and sound professional. When the text is clear and simple, and appears balanced on the page, the reader more easily grasps the message.

Some companies mandate a standardized format and font to ensure uniformity of company correspondence. If that's the case you are confronted with, find out if a business letter template is available. Use of a template will make it simple to follow the company format. If you don't have a template, follow basic business letter format. Type the recipient's address at the top left of the page. Skip a line and type the date. Start the letter with Dear Mr., Ms. or Mrs., unless you are very well acquainted with the recipient. Skip a line between each paragraph and close the letter with "Sincerely" followed by your name and title. Remember to focus on "you" instead of "I" or "we" in positive business letters and avoid "you" in negative ones.

❖ Make Your Point

Use the opening paragraph to briefly explain the purpose of the letter. Your first sentence might read, "A recent review of construction purchase orders revealed several cost overruns," or "We would like to offer you a 15 percent discount on your next printing job." State the purpose clearly and avoid jargon or highly technical language. If a secretary or assistant reads the recipient's mail, you'll want to make sure that a person understands the significance of your letter, even if he or she doesn't have a technical background.

❖ Be Detailed

Expand upon the first paragraph with more details. Short, concise letters might be more likely to be read, but enough details should also be provided, so that the recipient can fully understand the reason for the letter.

❖ Use Positive Words

Use positive words as much as possible and focus on what your company can do, rather than what it can't do. Keep in mind that the tone of your letter can affect the way the reader perceives it.

❖ End with a Request

Finish your letter with a request that asks the recipient to take some kind of action. For example, you might write, "Please provide me with the most recent cost projections by Tuesday," or "Call me to take advantage of your discount." Provide more than one way for the recipient to get in touch with you, such as a telephone number and an email address. Before you sign the letter and send it, be sure to review it for spelling and grammar errors.

Blocked Style vs Indented Style

Blocked style is a formal style which is common for business correspondences. It makes them easy and quick to read.

Every part or paragraph begins from the left margin, and all parts are typed single-spaced with a blank line between paragraphs. Two blank lines separate the date and the inside address, the address and the salutation, the salutation and the body, the body and the closing, and four blank lines between the closing words, such as "Sincerely yours," and the writer's printed name, which allows space for the signature.

The subject line is two blank lines below the recipient's address and two lines before the first paragraph.

Example Six

11, February, 2022

Jean Zhang
Haiyan Building 405
Dalian Software Park
Dalian, Liaoning Province
116023, China

                           Information for coconut oil

Dear Ms. Zhang,

The organic coconut oil displayed at Shanghai Agricultural Expo interests us. We would like to have your current catalogue, FOB Shanghai prices, and detailed information on discounts, delivery dates, and terms of payment.

As we are a leading dealer of imported foods in Alabama, USA, your competitive quotation may lead to possible long-term business relations.

I look forward to hearing from you soon.

Yours sincerely,

Kent Smith

Indented style is the traditional British practice with the heading usually in the middle and the date on the right-hand side.

All lines of an indented style begin from left margin with the exception of the first line of each paragraph in indented 4-10 spaces.

There is no blank line between paragraphs.

Whichever style you choose stick to it for the entire letter. Mixing up styles will make your letter look unprofessional. Its appearance will distract the reader from its content.

Example Seven

Cross Bridge Consultancy
121 Tidewater
AL 35758, USA

Millie Smith
1871 Beacon Street
Boston
USA

11, February, 2022

Dear Miss Smith,

Thank you very much for your invitation which I received yesterday. I shall be very happy to be part of your splendid event.

I shall make my own travel arrangement and be there on time.

Thank you again for your kind invitation and I look forward to seeing you soon.

Yours sincerely,

Oliver Liang

Samples for Appreciation

❖ Sample One Fax

FACSIMILE   **United Automation Corporation**

1874 Beacon Street
Tel: 31084708567
Fax: 31084708560

Receiver: Mr. Zhao Gang
Company: Dalian Deiseal Engine
Tel: 0086-411-86432098
Destination Fax: 0086-411-86432002

Dear Mr. Zhao,

Please kindly make arrangement to meet Mr. Ruffs, our engineer, who will arrive in Dalian by Flight CA 1865 on 11 January, 2022.

Please confirm receipt of the fax

Yours,

Chalet Ian

❖ Sample Two Email

To: Mr. Oliver An From: L. Chang
cc: Subject: thank you

Dear Dr. An,

I am absolutely happy to hear that you have joined us to help provide hands on support to people living with cerebral palsy and I wanted to write straight away and let you know how wonderful it is to have you on board.

Your regular gift of $25 will be put to good use, providing essential therapy and equipment to people living with cerebral palsy as well as helping our dedicated researchers uncover the very best treatment and interventions.

Thank you again for your amazing decision to help provide hands on support to people living with cerebral palsy. I know together we can achieve a great deal.

Best wishes,

Dr. Kent Jacob

❖ Sample Three Letter

Dear Dr. Zonk,

Your invitation for me to act as chairperson for the upcoming Space Science Conference is an honor. I had a wonderful time serving in that role last year.

At the moment I am working as a committee member of NSF that is taking up all my time. As much as I would enjoy working with you again, I am afraid that I wouldn't be able to give the duties the attention the project deserves.

I wish you and the conference great success.

Yours sincerely,

Ying

Tasks to Fulfill

scan for the keys

1. Can you answer the questions.

(1) What is business correspondence?

(2) What are the functions of business letters?

(3) How many standard parts are there in a business letter? What are they?

(4) How many optional parts are there in a business letter? What are they?

(5) Which do you think is the most important principle in business letter writing? Why?

2. Read and answer the following questions.

> Dear Prof. Lyon:
>
> I am very pleased to invite you to be a member of the review committee for the coming science competition to be held on 10th May in Rainbow High School.
>
> We will reimburse you for air travel and hotel accommodations. As a nonprofit association, we are unable to offer you an honorarium.
>
> Please let us know if you will be available for the event. Your feedback by 1st May is appreciated.
>
> Thank you.
>
> Sincerely yours,
>
> *Kate Spencer*
> President of Youth Development

Questions:

(1) What is the most important message?

(2) How much will Prof. Lyon be paid?

(3) Who will cover the traveling and hotel expenses?

(4) What is expected from Prof. Lyon before 1st May?

(5) Which words in the letter have a similar meaning to the following?

    A. contest   B. compensate   C. payment

3. Pease write an email on behalf of the University Facilities to all stuff based on the following details.

(1) Rainbow Elementary will be using Changchun Gym for their annual basketball match.
(2) It will be reserved for them on weekend, 8th May, 2022.
(3) Contact phone number: 31084706036.

Self-evaluation

1. Please put the phrases into English.

(1) 商务信函   (2) 信头   (3) 日期   (4) 称呼   (5) 落款
(6) 签名   (7) 传真   (8) 主题   (9) 电子邮件   (10) 抄送

2. You work for ABC Printing Company and have received instructions to print business cards for Ms. Wang, the marketing manager at Forest Guard Corp. The design work has been done and you need confirmation from Ms. Wang. Compose a fax about this.

No. 9 Baan Road, Shenzhen, China: 82776831 Fax 8675582777
To: (1)_____
Attention: Ms. Wang
Fax No.: 26435783

Fax from: Jin Nan
Date : 16 October, 2022

Subject: (2)_____

Ms. Wang,
(3)_____
_____.

If there are some places for improvement, let us know soon.

Looking forward to hearing from you.

3. Send a friend an email to tell him/her about your life and job in Shanghai. In it you ask about his/her plans for the National Holidays and invite him/her to visit Shanghai and share your apartment.

From: linda999@ yahoo. corn
To: lofts@ hotmail. com
Subject: Plan for the National Holidays

_____

How is everything with you? I hope things are going well.

_____
_____.

Best wishes,
Linda

4. Write a reply to the above email based on the information above.

From: lofts@ hotmail. com
To: _____
Subject: Reply to your invitation

Hi,
_____

All the best,
_____

5. **Complete the fax based on the following Chinese information. You can add other information that is not offered to you.**

假如你是保险公司的总经理助理 George Smith,发一份传真给国际贸易有限公司 Carl Zhang,问一下他是否收到一份你公司两周前 (2021年3月16日) 寄出的1715号订单的保险证,希望得到他的答复。

National Insurance Company
920 Broadway, New York, NY 12303

To: _____, 230 Royal Road, New York, NY 12350
Fax: 800-38562

From: _____
Fax: 800-50916

Date: _____
Page (s) : _____

Subject: _____,

_____
_____
_____.

All the best

Did you adopt the right layout for each of the correspondence?
Did you follow the right principle when writing them?
Did you avoid making grammar and spelling mistakes?

You can move on to Unit Two if you can complete the exercises satisfactorily.

Unit Two

Effective Business Writing

A business letter is an important form of technical communication. It is written primarily to state a specific purpose or message and eventually get a reaction or an answer from its receiver. It is different from the usual letters in that it appeals to reason rather than emotion. Business letters, often written by business people desiring to communicate with people other than their own close family and sent to people who are busy in their offices, are highly standardized.

Unit Objectives

After learning the unit, students should be able to compose effective business correspondences. They will:
1. Understand business writing styles;
2. Choose proper words;
3. Adopt a variety of sentence patterns;
4. Keep the paragraphs united and coherent ;
5. Present an appropriate overall tone.

Principles of Style to Follow

Business writing style means the way in which business ideas are expressed. It consists of the particular words the writer uses and manner in which those words are combined into sentences, paragraphs, and complete messages. According to Ober, the elements of an effective writing style include adaptation of proper words, a variety of sentence types, unified and coherent paragraphs and setting an appropriate overall tone (Ober 2006) .

❖ Choosing the Right Words

Words are basic units of sentences. Effective communication firstly depends on choice of proper words. You should keep the five principles in your selection of words: **accuracy, clarity, simplicity, concreteness, and conciseness.**

Accuracy

Firstly, it means freedom from spelling, punctuation, abbreviations, capitalizations, number expressions and grammar errors. Such careless mistakes leave readers a bad impression. All the above should all be checked carefully.

Secondly, it means you should be accurate

when addressing the receivers and offering such information as prices and specifications of measurements or weights.

Use the correct title in the address and salutation. Spell the receiver's name correctly, and write their address accurately. If the receiver's name and sex are unknown to you, you can use Dear Sir/Madam rather than Dear Sir or Dear Madam. If you know the name but not the sex, use Mr/Ms, for example, Dear Mr/Ms Wang. When replying to a letter, fax, or email, spell your correspondent's name correctly and write their address accurately. Take special care when offering quotations, as quoting incorrectly leads to serious consequences.

Thirdly, it means the writer gets the facts right. For example, consider the sentence from a business letter to a supplier:

I was shocked to find that your prices have now been increased by $300! To pay $580 for a coffee table that was $280 a few weeks ago is outrageous!

Suppose, in reality, the price of the commodity has been increased from $280 to $300, not by $300. The reader of the letter may wonder how trustworthy the writer is.

Clarity

Your message should be free from confusion in the aspects of abbreviations, numbers, and preposition.

Abbreviations are useful in that they are quick to write and easy to read. However, it has to be ensured that both the writer and the receiver know what the abbreviations stand for. For example, many people do know CIF stands for cost, insurance and freight, and L/C means letter of credit. But CCTV is different. It means Closed Circuit Television to some and China Central Television to others. If you are not absolutely certain that an abbreviation or set of initials will be easily recognized, it is best not to use it.

Besides, the use of figures instead of words for dates can also cause confusion. As a rule, the month in the date should be written in words, as figures can be confusing. For example, 12,09,20 means 12 September 2020 in British English, where the sequence is day-month-year, 09 December 2020 in American English, where the sequence is month-day-year, and 20 September 2012 (or 1912) in China, where the sequence is year-month-day.

Business writing contains numbers. Numerical expressions can also cause confusion. For example, the decimal point in British and American usage is a full stop, but a comma is used in most continental European countries, so that a British or American person would write 4.255 where a French person would write 4,255 (which to a British or American person would mean four thousand two hundred and fifty-five). If there is the possibility of confusion, write the expression in both figures and words, e.g. ¥10, 575.90 (ten thousand five hundred and seventy-five yuan, ninety fen).

Careless use of preposition leads to confusion. There is a huge difference between the two sentences "The price will increase to $260 per set." And "The price will increase by $260 per set."

Simplicity

Business writers focus on information. Their chief concern is to get the information correctly comprehended. Therefore, short, simple words are preferred as they are more likely to be understood.

> *Not: Company operations for the preceding accounting period terminated with a substantial deficit.*
> *But: The company lost much money last year.*
>
> *Not: The decision was predicated on the assumption that an abundance of monetary fund was forthcoming.*
> *But: The decision was based on the belief that there would be more money.*

Concreteness

Mistakes in business writings send a negative message about the writer's attitude and competence and may lead to serious misunderstandings. Special attention should be paid to spelling, capitalization, and punctuation. Special care should be taken when quoting prices or giving specifications such as measurements or weights.

Our prices were quoted in US dollars, not euros, which explained the difference of $263 in the June statement.

After looking into the matter, we found that the bed covers were ordered in metric sizes on our part and were made in British ones on your part.

We ordered and paid for 10 kilograms of butter; nevertheless, we received 10 pounds of butter. Please send us either the remaining butter or your credit note.

Conciseness

Business people are busy. Do not include unnecessary words in your business correspondence. Avoid redundancy.

> *Not: Please endorse on the back of this check.*
> *But: Please endorse the check.*
>
> *Not: Our salespeople are inexperienced. Consequently, we did not finish our quota.*
> *But: The inexperience of our salespeople causes us to miss our quota.*
>
> *Not: We have to turn down your order with regret. We are unable to dispatch your order within one month, as we have full order books now.*
> *But: We are sorry we cannot dispatch your order within one month due to the full order books we have.*
>
> *Not: We regret that we are unable to comply with your request to reduce the prices as our prices are closely calculated. Even if there is difference between our process and those of other suppliers, you will find it profitable to buy from us because the quality of our products is far better than any other foreign makes in your district.*
> *But: This is the best price we can offer. Our high quality justifies the quotation. You will find it profitable to buy from us.*

Besides, being concise also suggests that the writer use as few words as possible in communication.

Not:

> Dear Mr. Gary:
>
> I beg to acknowledge receipt letter of the 15th with regard to our not clearing our May account, which was outstanding since the end of the month.
>
> Please accept our profound apologies. The reason that the account remained outstanding was that we were moving to our new office in Madison and training new stuff to get familiar with our accounting system. We have now settled in the new office in Madison and started to clear all the outstanding accounts as quickly as we can. You will be glad to know that our bank has been instructed today to credit $ 3885.6 to your account, which I believe you will receive within 3 working days.
>
> We hope you can keep in mind the fact that we usually settle our accounts promptly and this is a rare exception, which was caused by our moving into a new office.
>
> Please check with your bank and let us know if the money has been credited to your account.
>
> Thank you.
> Yours sincerely,
> Ms Che

But:

> Dear Mr. Gary:
>
> Thank you for your letter of 15 July asking us to clear our May balance.
>
> We have instructed our bank to credit $3885.6 to your account today, and we apologize for not settling the account promptly, which was caused by our moving to the new office in Madison. We have fully trained stuff now and have settled in the new office. Future accounts will be paid promptly.
>
> I apologize for the inconveniences. Thank you for your patience.
>
> Yours sincerely,
>
> Ms Che

❖ Adopting a Variety of Sentence Types

There are four basic sentence types in English — simple, compound, complex and compound-complex. A combination of the four types helps build effective sentences.

• A simple sentence is one clause with a subject and verb, and it presents a single idea. It is often used for emphasis. A simple sentence may have a compound subject or compound verb, or both.

1. 1.5 percent on the unpaid balance will be charged.
2. Both the supplier and buyer agree to the terms of payment.

3. Bills are made on the 20th of each month and are payable by the 15th of the next month.

4. These documents are part of the contract for your deposit account and govern all transactions relating to your account, including all deposits and withdrawals.

• A compound sentence consists of 2 or 3 independent clauses, each receiving equal emphasis. In this sentence structure, the clauses are joined with such coordinating conjunctions as for, and, nor, but, or, yet, so.

1. China holds a huge market and great demand for development, and Japan holds advanced science and technology as well as enormous material force.

2. We have reminded you to dispatch the shirts (Order No 96396) by phone, fax, and email, but no logistics information of the order can be found yet.

3. Two packages were found lost in the consignment carried by the SS Tianjin, and garments to the value of $20,000 were found stolen.

4. The production is back to normal, so delivery is likely to be made within this week.

• A complex sentence is one with an independent clause and at least one dependent clause. The more varied and the more accurate your complex sentences are, the more effective you will be in the communication. Not all ideas are equally important. The more important idea is usually put in the independent clause.

1. It will be at least one month before we get our next delivery. **Adverbial Clauses**

2. We are completely out of stock of the raw material you required. **Relative Clauses**

3. We have pleasure in advising you that I have instructed my bank to credit £1,000 to your account with Bank of China, London in settlement of my invoice of No. 2 order. **Noun Clauses**

4. If this order is completed to our satisfaction, more orders will follow. **Adverbial Clauses**

5. If you think your statement or receipt is wrong or you need more information about an electronic transfer on the statement or receipt, telephone or write us as soon as you can. **Adverbial Clauses**

6. We sympathize with the problem you have been facing in clearing your balance of account. **Relative Clauses**

7. We hope you will accept D/P payment terms. **Noun Clauses**

• Compound-complex sentences are the same as complex sentences but they also have a simple (or compound) sentence before or after the "complex" part. They are made up of two independent clauses and one or more dependent clauses (or subordinate clauses). In a compound-complex sentence, we join the complex independent clause to the other independent clause in the same way as for normal compound sentences.

1. We insisted that this consignment be delivered to our customer by the end of October; however, it is October 10 already and they have not

received the goods.

2. We will try hard to produce a new consignment, and we hope that you can extend delivery to the end of next month.

3. We contacted several suppliers, but none have the materials you asked for.

4. If we take more than 10 business days to do this, we will credit your account for the amount that you think is in error, so that you will have use of the money during the time it will take to complete our investigation.

5. If you fail to notify us in writing of suspected problems or an unauthorized transaction within the time period specified in the deposit agreement, we are not liable to you for, and you agree not to make a claim against us for the problems or unauthorized transactions.

Keeping the paragraphs united and coherent

Paragraphs are groups of sentences having a common topic or main idea. Every sentence in a paragraph should support the theme of that paragraph. The main idea is often identified in the first sentence of the paragraph, which is known as the topic sentence, with other sentences supporting this main idea with additional information.

Paragraphs in business correspondences are expected to be unified and coherent. Unity is achieved when the sentences in the paragraph work together to develop a single idea consistently and logically, and coherence is realized when each sentence is linked smoothly to the sentences before and after it.

Not

> *1. Give your name, the name of the meeting you are attending and date that you will be traveling. 2. NRESS will be billed directly for air travel. 3. Travel Leaders Corporate is not allowed to purchase premium (business or first class) tickets. 4. Inform Travel Leaders Corporate that you are an NRESS meeting participant. 5. Travel Leaders Corporate will arrange for you to receive your ticket through electronic ticketing. 6. Please note that if the flights you have selected are more costly than comparable flights found by Travel Leaders Corporate, you will be required to pay the difference. 7. If you prefer to select your own flights, you may do so and then contact Ms. Ria Stevenson in the Travel Leaders Corporate office in order for Travel Leaders Corporate to book your reservations.*

The above paragraph lacks unity. The overall topic of the paragraph is about how an NRESS meeting participant could get the air ticket. So Sentence 4 would be the best topic sentence. And you may also find that Sentence 3 should be left out as it provides extra information which is not closely related to the topic. The most unified paragraph would be sentences 4-1-5-2-7-6-3.

But

> *4. Inform Travel Leaders Corporate that you are an NRESS meeting participant. 1. Give your name, the name of the meeting you are attending and date that you will be traveling. 5. Travel Leaders Corporate will arrange for*

> you to receive your ticket through electronic ticketing. 2. NRESS will be billed directly for air travel. 6. If you prefer to select your own flights, you may do so and then contact Ria in order for Travel Leaders Corporate to book your reservations. 7. Please note that if the flights you have selected are more costly than comparable flights found by Travel Leaders Corporate, you will be required to pay the difference. 3. Travel Leaders Corporate is not allowed to purchase premium (business or first class) tickets.

Coherence in a paragraph is achieved by using transitional words, pronouns, repetitions, and parallelism.

e.g.1

> To book your car, please follow the steps. *First*, please contact Ria Stevenson of Travel Leaders Corporate at (tmpnprs@tlcorporate.com) or call (844) 250-2008 or (919) 443-0367. Ria must book your reservation to ensure we get the corporate rate and that the cost of the rental is billed to Arctic Slope Technical Services, Inc. or ASTS, Inc. *Second*, you will receive a Budget confirmation number along with your travel itinerary. At the Budget counter,
> you will only need to give the agent the Budget confirmation number and your driver's license. *Finally*, NRESS will cover the cost of car and insurance for dates that you are in official travel status. You are required to attach a copy of the receipt to your expense report at the completion of your trip.

e.g.2

> If you think your statement or receipt is wrong or you need more information about an electronic transfer (e.g., ATM transactions, direct deposits or withdrawals, point-of-sale transactions) on the statement or receipt, telephone or write us at the address and number listed on the front of this statement as soon as you can. We must hear from you no later than 60 days after we sent you the FIRST statement on which the error or problem appeared.
>
> —Tell us your name and account number.
>
> —Describe the error or transfer you are unsure about, and explain as clearly as you can why you believe there is an error or why you need more information.
>
> —Tell us the dollar amount of the suspected error.

Transitional words, the words first, second, finally in the first example and the parallel structure in the second example serve as signals of step-to-step development, indicating where the message is headed and letting the readers know what to expect.

❖ Presenting an Appropriate Overall Tone

Tone refers to the writer's attitude toward both the reader and the subject of the message. Business writers should strive for an overall tone that is confident, courteous, and sincere; and uses emphasis and subordinations appropriately; that contains nondiscriminatory language; that stresses the "you" attitude; and that is enhanced by effective design. (Scot Ober, 2006)

Four of the main characteristics that make business communication effective are introduced in this unit.

Courtesy

A tone of courtesy builds goodwill for you and your organization and the message is more likely to be accepted by the reader.

> *Not:* It shall be viewed as a breach of contract if you fail to open the credit within the specific time agreed upon.
> *But:* It shall be viewed as a breach of contract if the credit is not opened within the specific time agreed upon.
>
> *Not:* You failed to pay on the due date.
> *But:* The account remains uncleared.
>
> *Not:* The machine broke down because you did not follow the instruction manual that accompanied it.
> *But:* Please recheck the instruction manual that accompanied the machine.

Nondiscrimination

Nondiscriminatory language treats everyone equally, avoiding bias and offenses.

> *Not:* When a customer needs service, it is his right to ask for it.
> *But:* A customer who needs service has the right to ask for it.
>
> *Not:* Old citizens are entitled to free bus rides in the city.
> *But:* Citizens above 65 years old are entitled to free bus rides in the city.

Positiveness

A positive tone builds a positive climate and goodwill and thus develops a positive relationship. Negative words such as *no, don't, regret, fail* should be avoided.

> *Not:* It is with regret that we reject your order, as we find that you tend to delay your payment.
> *But:* Only payment by cash in advance is accepted for the time being.
>
> *Not:* We cannot ship you the goods until we receive your check.
> *But:* We will ship you the goods within 24 hours of receipt of your check.
>
> *Not:* If you don't pay up by the final deadline of February 10, you'll be hearing from our collection officer and this will become a legal matter.
> *But:* To avoid collection proceedings, please send us your payment as soon as you can.
>
> *Not:* We regret to inform you that we cannot permit you to use our auditorium for your meeting, as the Ladies Investment Club asked for it first. We can, however, let you use our conference room, but it seats only 60.
> *But:* Because the Ladies Investment Club has reserved the auditorium for the weekend, we can instead offer you our conference room, which seats 60.

You attitude

The "you attitude" means looking at a topic from the reader's point of view ("you") instead of our own ("me"). "What's in it for me?" is the reaction of most people when they encounter a message. When business writers address their clients' or customers' self-interest first, there's a greater likelihood that the message will actually be read, the receiver will feel respected and cared for, and the message will help to forge a stronger business/customer relationship.

> Not: I have requested that your order be sent out today.
> But: You will receive your order by Wednesday.

> Not: In order to complete our inventory on time, we will be closing early on December 14th. Please plan to shop early on that day.
> But: We invite you to shop early on December 14th so we can meet your needs before our early closing.

> Not: We can allow a 20% trade discount if payment can be made within three weeks after receipt of the goods.
> But: You can take advantage of the 20% trade discount we offer to buyers who make payments within three weeks after receipt of the goods.

> Not: We are fulfilling your order and will have it ready by August 18.
> But: Your order for cabinets is in production, and will be delivered to you on August 18.

Sentence Patterns for Appreciation

Expressing emotions

1. I am afraid you will be very angry at the news. X   I am fully aware how frustrating the news is. √
2. You will be glad to know that the goods will reach you by the weekend. X   The goods will reach you by the weekend. √
3. You must be very angry that the goods ordered failed to reach you promptly. X   I am sorry for the late delivery. √

Expressing negation

1. We regret to inform you that we must deny your request for credit. X   For the time being, we can serve you on a cash basis. √
2. I cannot release the names of our clients. X   Releasing the names of our clients would violate their right to privacy. √

3. We can not ship you the goods until we receive your check. X
   We will ship you the goods upon receipt of your check. √

Adopting you-attitude

1. We close at 7 p.m. on Fridays. X
   We're open until 7p.m. on Fridays to give you time to shop after work. √

2. I cannot tell you the specific ingredients of herbal medicine. X
   Releasing the specific ingredients of herbal medicine would not be allowed. √

3. The machine broke down because you did not follow the instruction manual that accompanied it. X
   Please recheck the instruction manual that accompanied the machine. √

Being concise

1. Combine the ingredients together. X
   Combine the ingredients. √

2. Your order is very small, so we can not offer you any quantity discount. X
   Quantity discount is granted to orders up to $5000. √

3. The booklet, which is available free of charge, will answer your questions. X
   The booklet will answer your questions. √

Avoiding discrimination

1. Old citizens are entitled to free bus rides in the city. X
   Citizens above 65 years old are entitled to free bus rides in the city. √

2. When a consumer receives a faulty article, it is his right to get a new one. X
   A customer who receives a faulty article has the right to get a new one. √

3. Our Mexican driver delivered the ice-boxes to the wrong address. X
   Our driver delivered the ice-boxes to the wrong address. √

Samples for Appreciation

❖ Sample One Granting Request

Dear Applicant,

We are happy to inform you that the processing of your visa application is now complete. Your visa will be available through China Post, in 3 to 5 business days from the receipt of this email, either by pick-up or mail delivery.

Please note, effective Monday, December 28th, 2009, China Post will open its new branch office near the U.S. Embassy. All applicants should proceed to the new office to make arrangements for return of their passport and visa. China Post is located at No. 3 North Liang Ma Qiao Road, Chaoyang District. Tel: 6592-9907

❖ **Sample Two Offering an Appointment**

Dear Dr. Ruby,

I am pleased to offer you an appointment as a UCLA Postdoctoral Scholar Employee beginning August 1, 2020 and ending July 31, 2022. This appointment is assigned at 100% time with a monthly salary of $4375.00, less any deductions required by federal, state, or university regulations. Your appointment will be funded by NSF(211181) & NASA(21635). However, the university has discretion to change funding sources as necessary but will notify you of the change if it impacts your title or research project.

Please sign to indicate your acceptance of the position and return by May 15, 2020.

Sincerely,

UCLA Facilities

Issac James

❖ Sample Three Announcing Clearance of Parking Spaces

Dear all,

Remodeling Management Team informs that your parking spaces (17, 18, 19, 34, and 35) must be cleared between 8am-5pm on Monday, November 17, 2022, in order for contractors to pour concrete ramps for the ADA-compliance (American Disabilities Act) pathway to accommodate wheelchair(s), etc.

Found cars in these parking spaces will be ticketed or towed, if we cannot locate the residents when the work begins.

We realize this may be an inconvenience to request that you park on the street during this time (please look out for no-parking time zones and street cleaning day signs on street), and we appreciate your understanding and cooperation.

Sincerely,

James King

❖ Sample Four Replying to a Complaint

Dear Mr. Zonk,

Thank you for your email of February 11, 2022, informing me that 60 press washers were delivered to you.

We apologize for the mistake and meanwhile there are two options available at this time: you can keep the additional merchandise and we will bill you thirty days from now, or we will arrange to have it picked up at your loading dock and issue a credit note to you. Please let me know your preference.

Thank you for your patience.

Sincerely,

Millie

❖ Sample Five Replying to a Complaint

Dear Mr. Lee,

We respectfully draw attention to your June account, amounting to $6600 which is now considerably overdue for payment, and shall be glad if you will kindly send us your cheque by return.

It is regretted that no further goods can be supplied until the amount shown above has been settled in full.

If you have forwarded a remittance in settlement within the last few days, please disregard this letter.

Yours sincerely,

Lady Patricia King

Tasks to Fulfill

scan for the keys

1. Can you answer the questions?
(1) What are the five key standards in word choice?
(2) What are the four basic English sentence types?
(3) What can you do to keep a paragraph united and coherent?
(4) What is the overall tone one should adopt for business writing?

2. Please read the passage and answer the questions.

> The diversity of Niagara's natural and sustainable areas sets it apart from other vacation destinations. There are hundreds of outdoor experiences waiting for you. Niagara parks, gardens and conservation areas are sure to inspire and delight. Whether you are looking for a beachfront park, a picnic area or somewhere that allows you to experience the escapement, we have it all. Niagara's natural habitats offer rock cliffs, waterfalls (not just the Niagara Falls), wildlife and species rarely seen in Canada thanks to our temperate climate. No matter if you are a first-time explorer or a seasoned nature lover, you'll be invigorated by Niagara's vibrant nature.

Questions:
(1) What is the topic sentence?
(2) Why do you think "you" are adopted in several sentences?
(3) What distinguishes Niagara from other holiday destinations?
(4) What are the two major parts of this resort?
(5) Which words in the letter have a similar meaning to the following?
　A. make you happy　B. waterside　C. mild　D. experienced

3. Please translate the passage into English.

> 我厂坐落在风景如画的海滨城市大连，是国内规模比较大的贝雕工艺品厂，我们生产并销售各种手工贝雕工艺品，是馈赠亲友、喜庆致贺、表彰纪念的佳品。

Self-evaluation

1. Read and underline the main ideas.

（1）我们打交道以来，您总是按期结算货款的。可是您 L89452 号发票的货款至今未结。告知我方您是否遇到什么困难了。

（2）贵公司大概早已知道，我公司在出口贸易中历来只接受信用证付款。尽管如此，我方同意贵公司提出的分期付款的要求，即 50% 的货款用信用证支付，50% 的货款用承兑交单 60 天远期汇票付清。

（3）金叶系列的茶具由一级瓷土烧制，图案均为手工绘制，包装美观醒目，且现货供应。这个系列的产品非常适合您的市场。

（4）经过仔细的检查，我们发现实际重量和发票上的重量相差 35 公斤。

（5）等双方建立起稳定的关系且分销商证明了其盈利能力之后，我们可以考虑采用其他的支付方式。

（6）昨晚我厂发生了火灾，虽然最终扑灭，但是原计划后天发往你处的部分货物受损严重，无法按期交货了。

（7）我公司坐落在辽东半岛，是中国有名的水果出口地。

（8）我们在等待保险公司的赔付，一旦得到赔款，我们就全额结清您的欠款。

（9）您订购帐篷的时候只说了规格和款式，对颜色并没有具体的要求，所以我方才发给您各色帐篷各 6 个。

（10）与国内订单不一样，国际订单需要 6 周才能交货，这一点我们已经在产品目录里讲得很清楚了。

（11）物价飞涨，从下个月开始我们的门票价格将由 60 元涨至 100 元，望周知。

（12）为庆祝我厂成立 60 周年，由厂工会主办的运动会将于 5 月 26 日上午 9 时在市体育场举行。特邀请您莅临指导。

（13）由于我公司将搬迁至翰茨维尔，在随后的三周内可能无法及时回复您的信函。

（14）三山岛和海南岛的面积差不多，那里气候温和，风光优美，适合发展旅游业。

（15）这个机器在最近的 10 天内坏了 5 次，平均 2 天坏一次，我们要求退货。

2. Please translate the sentences into English.

（1）很高兴收到您 4 月 5 号的来信。

（2）我们的报价是每一百件 160,000 日元。

（3）请您务必月底交货。

（4）工程无法按期完工您一定很恼火。

（5）收不到您 30% 的预付款我们不会开始生产。

（6）因维修需要，明天 8 点至 16 点停车场不得停车。

（7）游客止步。

（8）如你方没有在约定的时间内开好信用证，这将被视为违约。

（9）我们的价格已经精打细算，没有降价的空间了。

（10）我方保证下个月发送的产品和你们刚才所见到的样品在质量上不会有差别。

（11）除非全额结清上文提及的欠款，否则我们停止给您供货。

（12）使用手册上写着不能在户外使用。

（13）您的订单并没有说不要红色的毛衣。

（14）这个等级的海参每斤涨到人民币 3200 元了。

（15）您现在明白了吗？

3. Can you make the sentences more effective?

(1) You have to make shipment before May 16, 2021 which is the firm condition of the order.

(2) We cannot offer you any quantity discount as your order is not large enough.

(3) You made a calculating mistake in your June account. We hope you can correct it immediately.

(4) You didn't enclose the price list in your letter.

(5) If a customer fails to pay on the due date, he is faced with a late payment fee.

(6) We will open at 9 am.

(7) We agree to reimburse you.

(8) The machine broke down because you did not follow the instruction manual that accompanied it.

(9) We have been quite tolerant of your and must now cancel our order with you.

(10) We do not offer credit facilities to initial buyers.

(11) You did not pack the goods as per our instruction; as a result, six of the plastic basins are crushed.

(12) We cannot offer you either a replacement or refund.

(13) If you fail to pay on the due date, you will face a late payment fee.

(14) The new line is very popular in the low-income areas, according to our survey of 200 families in Northeast China.

(15) Please do not park your cars in the parking spaces. If you do, your cars will get tickets or towed.

Did you pay enough attention to your choices of words?
Did you adopt a variety of sentence patterns?
Did you avoid offensive language?
Did you build goodwill by being courteous?
Did you apply you-attitude in your communication?

4. Can you produce an appropriate English version of the following passage?

> 贝雕九龙壁，全长 7.15 米，宽 0.73 米，高 2.75 米。整个作品由大连贝雕公司历时三年多完工。该九龙壁以北京北海公园大型九龙壁为蓝本，结合贝雕工艺的特点精制而成。制作团队选择使用了重两吨，共十五种贝壳为原料制作出了该九龙壁，其中包括大、小龙共 1595 条、元宝花 1048 个、斗拱 104 个。

Did you have a topic sentence?
Did you position the topic sentence in the right place?
Did you use a variety of sentence patterns?
Did you build goodwill by means of you-attitude?

You can move on to Unit three if you can complete the exercises satisfactorily.

Unit Three
Enquiry

An enquiry is a request for business information, such as price lists, catalogues, samples, and details about the goods or trade terms. It is usually made by the importer, but can be made by the exporter. On receiving the enquiry, it is a regular practice that the exporter should reply to it without delay.

People write business letters and emails for a variety of reasons such as requesting information, to conduct transactions, to secure employment, and so on. Effective business correspondence should be clear and concise, respectful in tone, and formatted properly.

Unit Objectives

After learning the unit, students should be able to:
1. Understand structure and content of business enquiries;
2. Recognize and remember related expressions and sentence patterns of business enquires;
3. Apply the above in their business enquiries.

Structure & Content

A typical enquiry contains three sections, an introduction, a body, and a conclusion.

The introduction tells who the writer is addressing. It usually contains a brief reason of why you're writing. A typical introduction includes only a sentence or two in length.

The letter's body is where you state your business. The length varies from a few sentences to several paragraphs based on the degree of detail necessary to describe the subject at hand.

The conclusion is the final section where you make clear what you would like from your reader. It should be no more than a sentence or two.

Expressions to Learn and Remember

Terms to remember

Price information	catalog, price list; current/latest/*outdated* catalog/price list; quote/offer a price; *FOB/CIF* Dalian/Main *European* ports; *net/gross price*; ex-works
Advertising material	brochure/*booklet, prospectus, leaflet*; samples, *patterns*; demonstration/show/display/showroom visits
Discount and commission	ask for and allow/give/offer a discount/commission; cash discount, quantity discount, trade discount; anniversary discount, commission off/on the net/gross price
Term of payment	ask for goods on approval; on sale or return basis
Enquiry	make an enquiry/enquire about a product; ask about the prices; ask for a price list/a catalogue with a price list/the list(ed) prices.

Sentence Patterns for Application

Introducing or referring to yourself

1. Our company is one of the main producers of bicycles based in Qingdao.
2. We are a subsidiary of the ABC Co. Ltd.
3. We are (particularly) interested in the black tea you are advertising on CCTV.
4. We would like to establish business relations with buyers from Eastern Asia.
5. We were impressed by the selection of your products displayed at your stand at the fair/exhibition held in Dalian last year.
6. We are in search of latest, sturdy and durable products for our chain hotels.
7. With reference to your advertisement in *China Daily*, we would like to know more about leather bags.
8. I'm following up on our telephonic conversation last Wednesday.
9. You were recommended to us by Prof. Larry Lyon of UCLA.

Asking for catalogue, price-lists, and details

1. Could you please send us your current / latest / up-to-date summer catalogue and price list, quoting the best/lowest prices CIF Dalian?
2. Would you let us have your prospectus / brochure for holidays in Xizang in summer?
3. I am writing to inquire about the dinner sets you are offering at cost price.
4. We would like to know if you offer any trade discounts.
5. We would be grateful if you could quote us your most competitive FOB Dalian price.
6. I would appreciate it if you could tell us more details about the discounts you can offer.
7. Could you supply details of the latest design of your product?
8. Please send us any information you can supply.
9. I would like to know more about the oil you are offering at cost price.

Suggesting terms of payment, including discounts

1. We usually deal on a 30% trade discount basis with an additional quantity discount.
2. We would appreciate it if you could let us know if you allow any credit facilities.
3. We mainly settle our accounts on a D/A basis with payment by 30-day B/E.
4. As a rule suppliers allow/give us a quantity/cash discount.
5. We would like to know if you allow cash or trade discounts.
6. What quantity discount do you offer?
7. If the concessions we asked for could be met, we would certainly place a substantial order.
8. If the product is satisfactory, we will place further orders with you in the future.
9. If the prices quoted are competitive, and the quality up to standard, we will order on a regular basis.

Asking for samples, patterns, demonstrations

1. When replying, could you enclose a pattern card/sample book?
2. Could you send us at least two examples?
3. We would appreciate it if you could send some sample materials.
4. I would be grateful if you could arrange for one of your representatives to call on me within the next two weeks.

Asking for trial sale

1. Your leaflet advertising goat milk interests us. We would like to stock a selection and see how our customers will react to them.
2. As we find your sports shoes attractive, we would like to try this new line out.
3. We are not certain about customers' reaction. We would be glad to hold a stock and see how it sells.
4. We would prefer to stock a selection on an approval basis for three months.

Encouraging further contacts

1. I would be grateful for your early reply.
2. Please contact us again if we can help in any way.
3. If you have any questions, feel free to call me.
4. You can also use the closing to request or offer future contact with the reader.
5. I look forward to hearing from you soon.
6. Please contact my assistant to schedule an appointment.

Samples for Appreciation

❖ Sample One Asking for Information

Dear Sir or Madam,

My name is Alice and I'm writing to you on behalf of Madison Entertainment. I would like to inquire about the sports facilities you produce, esp. in the range of treadmills. I would like to have an idea about the different models, features, and options available. Also please tell me if you offer any discount for bulk orders.

Your prompt reply will be appreciated.

Faithfully,

Alice Lin
Daily Articles Division

❖ Sample Two Asking for Information

Dear J. Wong,

I am writing to enquire whether you could send me details of the local tours your company provides. I would also be grateful if you would be able to send me information about your one-day tours.

Your tours were recommended by Mr. K.K. Chan of Fortune Trading. Mr. Chan used your company to organize a staff outing for his staff, and I would like to do the same.

I look forward to hearing from you.

Yours sincerely,

David Choi

General Manager

❖ Sample Three Asking for Information

Dear Sir or Madam,

Enquiry about Quality Control Course

I am writing to enquire whether your company could offer a course on Cross-culture Communication Skills for our managers.

I saw your advert in the *HK Daily* on Wednesday, 24 June 2020, and the Cross-culture Communication Skills (Ref.: QC 101) mentioned in the advert might be suitable for us. I would like to know if it is possible for you to offer a 3-month training course starting before or, at the latest, on Monday, 13 July 2020, for a group of 20. Could you send us some information about the teaching staff and the possible schedule for this course?

I am looking forward to receiving your reply.

Yours faithfully,

Chapmen Au

Managing Directon

❖ Sample Four Request for Catalogue and Price List

Dear Sir or Madam,

Your company was recommended to me by Ms. Elsie Wong of Far Eastern Logistics. Our African customer is interested in importing a range of printed 100% cotton cloth.

Please send me your current catalogue, and price list FOB Guangzhou.

I look forward to hearing from you.

Yours,

K.K. Chan

Merchandiser

❖ Sample Five Asking for Details of Dairy Products

Dear Mr. Flintstone,

As we have learned from Zhong's, our business associate, you are *manufacturers* of cheese products in America.

We are a well-established retailer based in Shenzhen, with outlets throughout China. And right now we are in the market for dairy products. We would be grateful if you could send us full details about your products.

Besides, we would like to know your earliest date of delivery and on what term you can give us a discount, if you are prepared to grant discounts.

If your prices are competitive and your goods up to our standard, we shall order on a regular basis.

Yours sincerely,

Kenneth Beare

Director of Ken's Cheese House

❖ Sample Six Asking for an Offer

Dear Sirs/Gentlemen,

We are both wholesale and retail dealers in men's wear and are interested in the belts you manufacture. We believe these belts can become quite attractive on our Asian market, especially together with a new line of jeans we are marketing here.

We believe there's a great potential in marketing your belts. Therefore we would like to place an order with you for 200 belts as soon as possible. The belts should be of five various models or designs at least.

We would be very grateful if you could let us know by email or fax if you are able to deliver this quantity before the end of April this year.

Please send us an offer in USD or EURO as soon as possible.

We are looking forward to your reply with great interest.

Faithfully yours,

Earuy Smith

Unit Three Enquiry 49

Tasks to Fulfill

scan for the keys

1. Can you answer the questions?

(1) What should be included in an enquiry?
(2) What should the writer say at the beginning of the enquiry?
(3) What sort of information is usually asked for in an enquiry?
(4) What should be stated at the end of an enquiry?

2. Read and answer the following questions.

> Dear Sir/ Madam,
>
> We are a furniture manufacturer based in Alabama and are looking for a supplier who can supply us with a wide range of fabrics for the upholstering of our furniture. We were impressed by the materials displayed on your stand at the Dalian Textile Exhibition held last March.
>
> As we usually place large orders, we would expect a quantity discount in addition to a 20% trade discount off net list prices. Our terms of payment are normally 30-day bill of exchange, D/A.
>
> If these conditions interest you, and you can deliver within six weeks of receipt of orders, please send us your latest catalogue and price list, Miami, FL
>
> We hope to hear from you soon.
>
> Faithfully Yours,
>
> *Jerry Liang*
>
> Chief Buyer
> Gary & Co. Ltd

Questions:

(1) What products is Gary & Co. interested in?
(2) Where did Gary &Co. get to know about Dalian Fabrics?
(3) What kinds of discount are they asking for?
(4) How would payment be made?

(5) Which words in the letter have a similar meaning to the following?
   A. selection   B. presented   C. hope   D. current

3. Fill in the blanks to complete the letter.

> I am the chief designer of Double Tree Hotel. I am (1)_____ （写信请求）your interior designing catalogues for the hotel.
>
> Would you also (2)_____ （给我一些样品木料）for the hotel lobby and sample wallpapers for the guest rooms, together with the (3)_____ （价格单和交货日期）?
>
> Please arrange your representative to (4)_____ （联系我） and check out the details next week.
>
> (5)_____ （烦请尽快回复）.

Self-evaluation

1. Can you translate the following expressions into English?
(1) 产品目录   (2) 价目表   (3) 离岸价   (4) 招生简章   (5) 样品
(6) 行业折扣   (7) 询盘   (8) 成本价   (9) 连锁店   (10) 总部
(11) 批发商   (12) 厂家   (13) 详情   (14) 报价   (15) 宣传册
(16) 分店   (17) 交货日期   (18) 订单   (19) 建立贸易关系   (20) 经销商

2. Please translate the sentences into English.
(1) 我公司是一家大型连锁零售商店，总店设在伦敦，专营中国工艺品。
(2) 贵公司在大连交易会展台上展销的各种电子产品给我们留下了深刻的印象，请惠寄最新产品目录和价目表，报出最低大连抵岸价。
(3) 我们对于您厂的凉席很感兴趣，能否给我们寄来两个样品？
(4) 如果质量达到我方要求，我们将大量订购。
(5) 销售旺季马上就要到了，请您尽快复函，说明您的付款方式、折扣详情和最快的交货日期。
(6) 我厂实力雄厚，历史悠久，长期需求高品质煤炭。
(7) 烦请您用电子邮件或传真告诉我方贵厂是否能在 6 月底供应三种不同款式的皮带共计 400 条？
(8) 我们与我们在英国的客户建立了牢固的关系，并打算派 30 名员工参加贵校的商务英语课程。请告知我们贵校开学时间及课程详情。

（9）贵厂接到订单后多久交货？

（10）我们对您在《中国日报》上宣传的机械设备很感兴趣，烦请提供更多详情。

（11）我们是一家国有公司，有 60 多年的历史，专营轻工产品。

（12）我们的商业伙伴对你们生产的糖果赞誉有加，我们很感兴趣，请您惠寄带有图片的最新的产品目录和价目表。

（13）我方欲购该书 200 册，请用欧元报价并告知你方对于交货前付款是否能提供现金折扣。

（14）我方对顾客的反馈尚无把握，想试销 3 个月。

（15）我们的供货商通常允许我们先拿货后付款，即月底结算。如您需要，我们可以提供资信证明。

Did you make any grammar mistake?
Did you make any spelling mistake?
Did you apply the correct business words and adopt proper patterns in your sentences?

3. Please translate the sentences into Chinese.

(1) Your address was given to us by a company in Madison, AL.

(2) Please quote us your lowest price, stating the terms of payment and the packing materials used for the wine.

(3) Could you send us your quotations and let us know the terms and conditions of payment?

(4) We are a well-established retailer based in Hong Kong, with outlets throughout China.

(5) We were impressed by the selection of your products displayed on your stand at the fair/exhibition.

(6) Do you allow open account terms?

(7) We would be very grateful if you could let us know if you are able to deliver this quantity before the end of this coming April as soon as possible.

(8) We are both wholesale and retail dealers in men's wear.

(9) Your leaflet advertising goat milk interests us. We would like to stock a selection and see how our customers will react to them.

(10) If the prices quoted are competitive, and the quality up to standard, we will order on a regular basis.

(11) Please send us your quotation in euro by email or fax.

(12) Late deliveries will be rejected.

(13) We would like to know your earliest date of delivery and on what term you can give us a discount, if you are prepared to grant a discount.

(14) We would like to try this new line out.

(15) As sales season is only a few weeks away, delivery must be made within the time specified.

4. Can you write an English enquiry according to the details given below?

(1) Retailer in sports facilities.
(2) Impressed by the goods displayed at Shanghai Expo.
(3) Detailed information including models colors, prices, bulk order discounts, warranty, delivery.
(4) Long-term partnership.
(5) Look forward to an early reply.

Did you introduce who you are, how you got to know the product?
Did you mention what information you want in your enquiry?
Did you encourage further contact at the end of the enquiry?

You can move on to Unit Four if you can complete the exercises satisfactorily.

Unit Four
Replies and Quotation

When you receive a request for information concerning your products, you are expected to reply without delay. In addition to providing the information asked for, you also stress certain selling points of the products in the reply. A quotation is the repetition of a sentence, phrase, or passage from speech or text that someone has said or written. In business context, it is a document that lists the prices proposed by a seller for their goods or services and offered to a potential customer.

A quotation is not necessarily legally binding, i.e. the company does not have to sell the goods at the price quoted in the reply to an enquiry, but suppliers generally keep to firm offers to protect their reputation.

Unit Objectives

After learning the unit, students should be able to:
1. **Understand structure and content of replies and quotations;**
2. **Recognize and remember the related expressions and sentence patterns;**
3. **Apply the above in their business activities.**

Structure & Content

In a typical reply, the writer usually provides the information asked for, mentions the selling points, suggests an alternative if the product asked for is out of stock, and refers the customer to another supplier. The writer also states whether the catalogues, price lists, prospectuses, and samples are being sent and demonstrations and visits are being arranged.

In the opening part of your reply, appreciate the prospective customer's interest in the product or service by beginning the letter with his or her name, for example "Dear Mr. Lyon" or "Dear Ms. Zonk". Mention the date of his or her letter and quote any other references. Tell the receiver early in your reply whether you can help.

A quotation is a good opportunity to sell your products. It is simply not enough to provide the information requested. You should also mention one or two selling points of your product, including perhaps any guarantees you offer so as to encourage or persuade your prospective customer to do business with you. If what the enquirer has asked for is out of stock, you can offer him/her an alternative. And if you are not able to handle the order but know where he can get help, you may refer him/her to the supplier who can help.

In addition to giving quotations of prices and delivery dates, you may also mention the discounts allowed for and suggest methods of payment.

When closing the reply, writers are expected to encourage further enquiries from the possible buyers.

Example One

Dear Mr. Crane,	
We were pleased to receive your enquiry and hear that you liked our sweaters. Enclosed you will find our summer catalogue and price list.	Acknowledging receipt of enquiry & mentioning catalogue & price-list are enclosed
The usual allowance for a trade discount in our country is 25%, and we can offer you a 5% quantity discount for orders over $5,000. For initial buyers, we always deal on payment by sight draft, cash against documents. As we can supply from stock, there would certainly be no trouble in meeting your delivery date.	Answering questions asked
We are sure you will find a ready sale for our products in England.	Stressing selling points
Thank you for your interest. We look forward to hearing from you soon.	Encouraging further contacts
Yours sincerely,	Complimentary close
Jerry Liang	Signature

Example Two

Dear Ms. Ella Simpson,	
We were very pleased to receive your enquiry of 11 May and have pleasure in enclosing our latest catalogue and price list.	Acknowledging receipt & mentioning enclosures
Also by separate post we are sending you two sample gloves. We are confident that you will find our gloves excellent in quality and reasonable in price. Please note that our gloves can be made as per your specifications.	Telling samples are forwarded / Mentioning selling points
If there is additional information you would like to know, please feel free to contact us. We will be most happy to be of help to you.	Encouraging further contacts
Sincerely yours,	Complimentary close
Thomas Hall	Signature

Expressions to Learn and Remember

Terms to remember

Price information	price list; gross price; net price; purchase price; FOB/CIF Dalian/Main European ports; costs of transport/insurance; delivery charges; VAT; rate of exchange; currency
Discount and commission	offer/allow cash discount; quantity discount; trade discount; anniversary discount; commission off/on the net/gross price; loyalty discount
Term of payment	prefer cash in advance; allow open account facilities; installment payment; documents against payment; documents against acceptance; letter of credit; payment by irrevocable letter of credit; bill of exchange; sight draft; carriage paid; carriage forward
Delivery	meet the delivery date; guarantee delivery; deliver within the time specified; offer door-to-door delivery service; arrange freight and insurance

Sentence Patterns for Application

Thanking the customer for his/her enquiry

1. Thank you for your enquiry of 7 July in which you asked about our black tea.
2. I would like to thank you for your enquiry of 6 November.
3. Thank you for your letter which we received yesterday.
4. We were pleased to learn from your letter that you are impressed with our selection of printed silks.
5. Thank you for your interest in our woolen sweaters displayed on our stand at 16th Dalian Fashion Festival.
6. We were glad to know that you find our range of garden furniture attractive. Thank you for your interest in them.

Confirming that you can help

1. We can confirm that there would certainly be no trouble in supplying you from our wide selection of garments.
2. I am pleased to tell you that we would be able to supply you with 600 washing machines.
3. We have a wide selection of dinner sets that suit the market you specified.
4. I am pleased to say that we will be able to supply the mountain bicycles mentioned in your enquiry.
5. We provide school uniforms of all seasons that appeal to all ages.
6. We can supply from stock and will have no trouble in meeting your delivery date.
7. As a well-established company with abundant resources, we have no problem in turning out the 3,000 pieces you asked for.

Stressing the advantages of the product or service

1. We offer a wide range of products which are beautiful in design, high in quality, and competitive in price.
2. Irrigation Easy 730 is the most outstanding system on the market with its trouble-free performance and life-long guarantee.
3. We are sure that you will agree that our wall papers are the best once you see the samples enclosed.

4. The new model is made of plastic, which means it saves on oil and electricity.
5. With fewer moving parts, our robot cleaners need little maintenance.
6. With our outlets all over the whole world, we can promise you an excellent product with a first-class service.
7. We would like to draw your attention to the quantity discount we offer to bulk buyers.
8. Orders can be met as per your specifications.
9. You will find our service reliable and helpful as our technical and sales staff are always keen to provide information on all our products.
10. We have long been *recognized* as one of the *leading* manufacturers of domestic heating products, with over 60 years' experience in the design and *innovation* of heating appliances.

Quoting prices, business terms & delivery date

- **Terms of payment**
1. The terms of payment are the subject of negotiations.
2. We prefer payment by irrevocable letter of credit.
3. Normally we allow a 25% trade discount off net/gross prices with payment on a document against payment basis.
4. Credit facilities are offered only to customers who have established a firm relationship with us.
5. For initial and orders, we insist on payment by L/C.
6. 30% of the contract value shall be paid in advance by cash, and 70% by D/P at sight.

- **Discount**
1. Customers who pay within 7 days of receipt of invoices can enjoy a 3% cash discount.
2. Because of the low price and small profit margin, we will not be offering any trade discounts on this consignment.
3. All list-prices are quoted FOB Shenzhen and are subject to a 25% trade discount with payment by letter of credit.
4. You are welcome to take advantage of the 5% anniversary discount we are offering on all orders placed during June.
5. In addition to the 25% trade discount off list prices, we also offer to our retailers and wholesalers a quantity discount for orders over ¥,20,000.00.

- **Delivery**
1. Delivery by November can be guaranteed.
2. We can deliver within two weeks of receipt of order.
3. On receipt of a check for the amount quoted, we will send the article by registered mail.
4. As there are regular sailings from Shanghai to New York, we are sure that the consignment will reach you well within the time you specified.

- **Encouraging further contacts**
1. Please contact us again if we can help in any way.
2. If you have any questions, feel free to call me.
3. You can also use the closing to request or offer future contact with the reader.
4. I look forward to hearing from you soon.
5. Please contact my assistant to schedule an appointment.

Suggesting an alternative or referring his/her to others who may help

We no longer offer Business English Courses. We suggest you contact Dalian University of Technology, who provides Business English Training regularly.

Samples for Appreciation

❖ Sample One Reply to an Enquiry

Dear Mr. Zink,

Thank you for your enquiry of 31 January. We enclose our Spring Catalogue and current price list quoting FOB prices Qingdao.

We have long been recognized as one of the leading manufacturers of mowers in China, with over 60 years' experience in the design and innovation of cutting appliances.

Please contact us if we can be of any further help.

Yours sincerely,

Mr. Zhang Zhizhong

Sales Manager

❖ Sample Two Reply to Inquiry about Specification

Dear Mr. J. Wong,

Thank you for your letter of 29 September in which you inquire about our cotton cloth. We are sending you samples of B5 by airmail separately. The particulars of item B5 are:

Description	100% cotton	width 122 cm
Price	USD 0.60 (60 cents)	per meter
Terms of delivery	fas New York	
Mode of delivery	by ship	
Packing	in cases	90 x 80 x 50 cm
Time of delivery	4 weeks	
Terms of payment	Cash against documents	
Offer valid through	March 1, 2004	

Minimum order is 100 meters of each item.

We believe you will find the price very competitive especially considering the high quality of this article.

Additional information regarding our products is given in the enclosed brochures.

If there is any further information you need, please contact us, or go to our website at the address above.

We are looking forward to hearing from you.

Once again thank you for your enquiry.

Your sincerely,

Ms. Zhai Jiaxin

❖ Sample Three Reply to Inquiry

Dear Mr. Fisher,

Thank you for your inquiry regarding the Happy Walker. We are pleased to enclose our latest brochure.

The well-illustrated brochure describes all of the features that make the machine the most advanced total-body fitness equipment and the best-selling treadmill on the market. Our company also has an excellent reputation for quality, reliability, and service. We would very much like to add your clients to our worldwide list of customers, and could promise them an excellent product with a first-class service.

All our prices are quoted CIF to Amsterdam and are subject to a 23% trade discount off all net prices, with delivery within three weeks from receipt of order. Payment for initial orders is to be made by 45-day B/E, irrevocable L/C.

We would be glad to accept orders for any number of pieces.

If there is any further information you need, please contact us. Once again thank you for your interest in our health care products enquiry.

Yours sincerely,

David Choi
General Manager

❖ Sample Four Offer of Business Terms

Dear Mr Crane,

We were pleased to receive your enquiry and to hear that you liked our range of sweaters. We can confirm that there would certainly be no trouble in supplying you from our wide selection of garments.

We can offer you a quantity discount, which would be 5% off net prices for orders over £2,000, but the usual allowance for a trade discount in Italy is 15%, and we always deal on payment by sight draft, cash against documents. However, we would be prepared to review this once we have established a firm trading association with you.

Enclosed you will find our summer catalogue and price list quoting prices CIF London. We are sure you will find a ready sale for our products in England, as have other retailers throughout Europe and America, and we hope very much that we can reach agreement on the terms quoted.

Thank you for your interest. We look forward to hearing from you soon.

Yours,

Larry King

❖ Sample Five Reply to Promote Courses

Dear Ms. Iwanami,

Please find enclosed our prospectus covering courses from July to December. Details of fees and accommodation in London for that period are covered in the booklet 'Living in London' which accompanies the prospectus.

At present we still have places available for students taking the English for Business Executives course beginning in July, but would ask you to book as soon as possible so that we can reserve a place for you and arrange accommodation with an English family.

We are sure you will enjoy your stay here and look forward to seeing you.

Yours sincerely,

Kenneth Beare
Director of Ken's Cheese House

❖ Sample Six Reply and Offer of Samples

Dear Mr. Church,

We were very pleased to receive your enquiry of 11 May and have pleasure in enclosing our latest catalogue and price list for your reference.

Also by separate post we are sending you some sample gloves. We are confident that you will find our goods both excellent in quality and reasonable in price. We invite you to consider and compare the quality and price of our products, and look forward to receiving your first order.

If you have any further questions please do not hesitate to contact us at any time.

If there is additional information you would like to know regarding our products, please do not hesitate to contact us. We will be most happy to be of assistance.

Sincerely,

Sarah Biden

Tasks to Fulfill

scan for the keys

1. Can you answer the questions?

(1) What is an offer/quotation?
(2) What should be included in a reply?
(3) When should you let your reader know whether you can supply him/her in the reply?
(4) What are you expected to express at the end of the reply?

2. Read and answer the following questions.

Dear Mr. Stone,

We thank you for your inquiry about our cotton shirts.

We are a well-established manufacturer of children's garments. Enclosed you will find our catalogue together with prices and terms. The catalogue will provide many of the details of our products that you may interested in.

We are also pleased to inform you that we will allow you a 10% discount on order of 60 pieces.

Should you need more information about our products, terms of payment, methods of delivery, we would be happy to provide them straight away.

We hope you will find our prices and terms satisfactory and expecting your order as soon as possible.

Yours sincerely,
Paul Smith

Questions:

(1) What is enclosed in the letter?
(2) What sort of information can be found from the catalogue?
(3) Does the supplier offer any discount?
(4) What should Mr. Stone do if he wants to know details of payment?
(5) Which words in the letter have a similar meaning to the following?
    A. asking for information   B. producer   C. straight away

3. Please translate the sentences into Chinese.

(1) We would be glad to accept orders for any number of pieces, and can mix sets.

(2) We have the materials in stock and will ship them the moment we receive your order.

(3) As there is a heavy demand for heaters at this time of year, please allow at least six weeks for delivery.

(4) As you are responsible for the damage, replacements will be sent to you, carriage forward.

(5) In view of your long association with our company, we can offer you 12% off the retail price.

(6) In addition, we give a discount of 3% for payment made within fourteen days from date of invoice.

(7) We would be glad to accept orders for any number of pieces, and can mix sets if required.

(8) We can quote you a gross price, inclusive of delivery charges, of ￥200 per 10 items.

(9) The net price of this table with 4 chairs is $600, to which VAT must be added at 17.5%, making a gross price of $705.

(10) We have long been recognized as one of the leading manufacturers of domestic heating products, with over 60 years' experience in the design and innovation of heating appliances.

(11) Attached you will find our current catalogue and price-list, FOB Tianjin. Sample bicycles will be forwarded to you immediately when the shipping cost is received.

(12) The prices quoted are ex-works, but we can arrange freight and insurance if required. However, unless otherwise stated, payment should be made by 30-day bill of exchange, documents against acceptance.

(13) Enclosed you will find our latest catalogue and FOB Tianjin price-list. Goods will be dispatched within one week of receipt of the order and reach you within four weeks.

(14) Our vehicle tires have achieved excellent results in rigorous factory and track tests. They provide value for money.

(15) As a well-established company with abundant resources, we have no problem in turning out the 3,000 pieces you asked for.

Self-evaluation

1. Can you translate the following phrases into English?

(1) 随函寄上　　(2) 付款方式　　(3) 账期　　　　　(4) 交货日期

(5) 现货供应　　(6) 实力雄厚　　(7) 三年保修　　　(8) 汇率波动

(9) 付款交单　　(10) 即期汇票　　(11) 不可撤销信用证　(12) 保险

(13) 运费已付　　(14) 物美价廉　　(15) 欧元　　　　　(16) 立刻畅销
(17) 免除增值税　(18) 下订单　　　(19) 建立贸易关系　(20) 现金交单

2. Please translate the sentences into English.

(1) 您 6 月 6 日的来函我公司已收到，感谢您欲购我公司的产品，现随函寄上现行价目表一份。所报价格皆为离岸价。

(2) 我们从业 60 余年，在客户中享有良好的口碑。我们质量高，价格低，交货及时。

(3) 我们可以供应并负责安装管道和喷头，工料保修 8 年。

(4) 所附报价为净价，您可以享受 25% 的行业折扣。如订货超过 50 箱，另有 3% 的数量折扣。如果现金全额结清货款，还可进一步享受 2% 的折扣。

(5) 信中附有我厂生产的床单详情，另外，请注意，我们可以按照客户的要求定制。

(6) 除特别注明外，所作报价须经我方确认后方能生效。收到订单后，14 日内交货。

(7) 只有在双方建立稳定的贸易关系之后，我公司才可以提供账期。

(8) 新客户不享受账期。货款用即期汇票支付，见票付现金，支付地点为中国银行广州分行。

(9) 我们用美元结算。由于目前汇率变化很大，报价有效期为 3 周。

(10) 国内订单次日达，国际订单 4 周达，详情请见订购指南第 10 页。

(11) 信中附有最新的产品目录，详细介绍了产品的特点。

(12) 如果能提供资信证明，我们接受 30 天远期汇票承兑交单的付款方式。

(13) 所报价格均为南安普敦离岸价，可以享受七五折。

(14) 我们对新顾客，只接受信用证付款方式。

(15) 请注意，床单接受个性化定制。

3. Can you write a reply to a prospective buyer who has asked for detailed information about one of your products according to the details given below?

(1) We were pleased to receive the enquiry.
(2) Enclosed catalogue
(3) 25% trade discount, 5% quantity discount for orders up to $50,000, deliver within 4 weeks of receipt orders
(4) We are leading brand name, the best of its kind, sell well
(5) We will be happy to be of some help.

Did you use the customer's name rather than Dear Sir / Madam?
Did you let the customer know early whether or not you can help them?
Did you make sure that you have supplied all the information asked for?
Did you mention selling points?
Did you encourage further contact at the end of the offer?

You can move on to Unit Five if you can complete the exercises satisfactorily.

Unit Five

Counter-offer

More often than not you're going to find something in the buyer's purchase offer that you don't agree with. Maybe the offered price is too low, or the conditions and inclusions are too demanding. You are now presented with three options:

Acceptance

An accepted offer means you've agreed to all the terms and conditions exactly as set forth in the offer to purchase.

Rejection

Rejection means you turn down an offer when you do not agree with the terms (such as price) and conditions set forth in the offer to purchase.

Counter-offer

Prepare a counter-offer when you agree with some of the terms and conditions in the buyer's offer, but not all of them. The counter offer may change the price or closing date, or it may add or delete conditions.

A Counter-offer is virtually a partial rejection of the original offer and also a counter proposal initiated by the buyer or the offeree. They are prevalent in many types of business negotiations, transactions, private and public deals between two individuals or two entities. You may find them in real estate deals, employment negotiations, car sales, private placements, mergers acquisitions, takeovers, etc.

There is no limit to the number of times each party can counter during negotiations. When countering back and forth, each offer should present a price less than the previous offer, until both parties reach an agreement on a binding contract.

In business communication, it is important that the parties involved be polite and collaborative in any dealings. Try to communicate your own wishes clearly. Remain respectful when disagreeing with or rejecting your clients. Be patient and helpful when misunderstandings do crop up.

Unit Objectives

After learning the unit, students should be able to:
1. Understand what a counter-offer is;
2. Negotiate prices and business terms;
3. Recognize and remember related expressions and sentence patterns;
4. Apply them in related business activities.

Structure & Content

The writer should first of all acknowledge receipt of the offer, and follow up with reasons or explanations before coming up with a counter offer. At the end of the communication, further contact is encouraged.

The goal, when you're countering a buyer's offer, is to get the best price and best terms possible. The main contents include negotiations on quality, quantity, packaging, price, delivering and terms of payment, etc.

A positive, polite and professional tone should be adopted throughout the negotiation. Both parties should conclude a negotiation feeling comfortable and happy with the agreement finally reached.

Example One

Dear Mr. Nick,	
Thank you for your offer of July 21, 2022.	Acknowledging receipt
We have examined the samples carefully and we are happy with the quality and pattern. However, payment by cash exerts a heavy burden on our cash flow situation. We would be grateful if you could allow us to settle by monthly statements. We can provide credit references if needed.	Expressing satisfaction & reason for counter offer / Counter-offering
As you know, we are a large and reputable chain retailer. If the request can be granted, you can expect regular orders from us.	Persuading the reader to accept counter-offer
If you have any inquiry or question, please email it or call us at 001-31050530.	Inviting further contacts
Yours sincerely,	Complimentary close
Kenny Brown	Signature

Example Two

Dear Mr. Nick,	
	Acknowledging receipt of samples
Thank you for the sample organic vegetables you sent us. They are what we are looking for.	
	Stating the reason for counter offer
All the business terms you quoted suit us well except one: the 20% discount, which is 10% lower than the average offered to us by other suppliers. As we usually place large orders, we would appreciate it if you can allow us a 30% trade discount. With competitive prices, your vegetables and fruit will sell very well in our market.	Counter offer Inviting favorable consideration
We look forward to hearing from you soon.	Inviting further contacts
Yours sincerely,	Complimentary close
Bill Armstrong	Signature

Expressions to Learn and Remember

Terms to remember

Counter-offer	entertain a counter-offer, accept the counter-offer,
Discount	accommodate the discount, offer a discount, trade discount, quantity discount, special discount, cash discount
Price	best price, rock-bottom price, reduce the price,
Delivery	shorten the delivery, speed up the delivery
Packing	gift box, gift wrapping
Payment	credit facilities, net 45, on approval, on sale or return basis

Sentence Patterns for Application

Negotiating prices

1. Our suppliers usually allow us a 25% trade discount, which is 5% higher than the one you offered.
2. We would place large orders if the 5% quantity discount is granted.
3. This is the best price we can offer, as we work on a fast turnover and low profit margins basis.
4. If the transaction is concluded on an FOB basis, instead of the CIF you suggested, and a further 10% discount on net prices is allowed, we will send you our official orders.
5. If you can lower the price to $60 each bottle and deliver 3,000 bottles within 4 weeks of receipt of order, please let us know by fax or email.
6. All our customers, regardless the quantity they buy, are offered a 23% trade discount.

Negotiating payment terms

1. We usually pay our suppliers in net 90.
2. Due to the fluctuation of the exchange rate, we insist documents against payment at sight.
3. Your latest facial recognition machines interested us; we would like to stock a selection on approval. However we would only consider placing an order if it is on the usual basis of sale or return.
4. We expect an additional 1.5 % discount for payment made within 3 days after invoice date.
5. Our terms of payment are normally 30-day bill of exchange, documents against acceptance.
6. As we prefer to pay cash on delivery, we hope you can reduce the price by 3%.

Negotiating delivery date

1. We received your order No. 659 for our silk masks today but regret that we are unable to fulfill the order since we cannot meet the delivery date mentioned in your letter.
2. Two months must be allowed for delivery, as we ourselves have to get raw materials and rely on our own suppliers.
3. As we need the goods urgently, can you deliver them within the next two weeks?
4. You will receive our regular orders if the prices quoted can be reduced by 5% and delivery can be shortened from six weeks to four weeks.

5. To ensure good quality, we ask our suppliers to deliver the raw materials within 24 hours.
6. Can you supply us with the goods within fourteen days receipt of our order?

Negotiating other terms

1. We have no object to your packing of the garments in cartons if you can guarantee that you will pay compensation when our clients cannot get indemnification from the insurance company.
2. Do you provide gift bags and ribbons for the earrings, necklaces, bracelets and pins?
3. The dinner sets should put into wooden crates, which are clearly marked with your castle logo for easy identification.
4. Once your annual turnover reaches $500,000, you would become our sole agent. We would expand your territory to the whole East of China.
5. We expect an annual advertising allowance of $5,000 so that we can popularize and push your shampoo to our customers.
6. Do you offer promotional allowances? If you do, in what forms?

Samples for Appreciation

❖ Sample One Request for Monthly Payment

Dear Mr. Qu,

Thank you for your prompt reply.

A view of your catalogue convinces us that we can establish a market for your art works in my country, and we are happy with your commission and delivery date. However, we usually ask our customers to pay us directly and we then remit the quarterly payment, deducting our commission, to our suppliers. If this is acceptable to you, we would like to try some pieces.

As you know, we are a large and reputable chain art gallery. If the credit facility can be granted, you can expect regular orders from us.

If you have any inquiry or question, please email it or call us at 44450530.

Regards,

Jama Kingsbury

❖ Sample Two Request for a Lower Quotation

Dear Janet,

Thank you for your comprehensive proposal which we received on 9 May.

We do appreciate your time and efforts put in the proposal and we overall are happy with your detailed plan to provide what we need.

We have a limited budget this year due to the weather. As much as I would love to have you as our supplier, your quotation in the above mentioned letter makes this impossible. If your bid could be 9 % lower at a final price of USD 161,500, I would like to give the contract to you.

I hope you find our offer acceptable and look forward to your prompt reply by 1 September, 2021.

Best regards,

Morgan Freeman

❖ Sample Three Request for a Bigger Discount

Dear Mr. Stone,

Your organic vegetables and fruit are what we are looking for. There is an increasing demand for healthy foods like yours.

All the business terms you quoted suit us well except one: the 20% discount, which is 10% lower than the average offered to us by other suppliers. As we usually place large orders, we would appreciate it if you can allow us a 30% trade discount. With competitive prices, your vegetables and fruit will sell very well in our market.

We look forward to hearing from you soon.

Yours sincerely,

Simon Max

❖ **Sample Four Request for a Sale on Approval**

Dear Mr. Smith,

Thank you for your current catologue and price list FOB Guangzhou.

In the catalogue we received from you, we saw that you are introducing a new line — camel milk in powdered form. While we understand its health benefits, we are not sure how our customers would react to this high-end product. However, we would like to try 10 boxes of 1 kilogram on an approval basis to see if we can encourage a demand. Three months would probably be enough to establish a market if there is one.

Your early reply will be appreciated.

Thank you.

Sincerely yours,

James Sun

❖ Sample Five Asking for a Lower Price

Dear Mr. Smith,

Thank you very much for both your offer of May 5 and the samples of men's shirts which we received today.

While appreciating the good quality of your products, we find your prices a bit too high for the market we wish to supply.

We have to point out that the men's shirts are also available in our market from several European manufacturers, and all of them are at prices from 10% to 15% below the price you quoted.

Such being the case, we have to ask you to lower your prices by 10%. As we usually place substantial orders, you may think it worthwhile to make a concession.

We look forward to your early reply.

Sincerely yours,

L. Crane

❖ Sample Six Negotiating Packaging

Dear Mr. Liang,

We are writing to you about the cartons in which you intend to pack the garments.

My colleagues and I examined the sample carton closely and found that they are not seaworthy. The insurance company might refuse compensation should any loss incur.

We suggest you ship the garments in wooden crates with each piece individually sealed in a plastic bag, as our other suppliers do. However, your cartons are acceptable to us if you will compensate our clients when they suffer any losses and fail to get indemnification from the insurance company.

Thank you and we look forward to hearing from you soon.

Yours sincerely,

Bright Chan

Tasks to Fulfill

scan for the keys

1. Can you answer the questions.

(1) What is a counter-offer?
(2) What should be included in a counter-offer?
(3) Should you start your counter-offer by picking fault with the seller?
(4) What's the appropriate overall tone for business negotiation?

2. Read and answer the following questions.

Dear Mr. Henry Kingsbury,

We are interested in the motor bikes you offered to us in your letter of 8 October.

While we agree that your motor bikes are high in quality and attractive in design, in our opinion the prices quoted in the letter are a bit too high. Similar products from other suppliers are 10% lower. Besides, motor bikes in my country usually enjoy a three-year warranty. In view of this, we would expect a reduction of 10% on net invoice totals, and an extension of your warranty from two years to three years. However, we are prepared to leave this matter open for discussion. If these conditions are acceptable, then we would be pleased to send our first order to you immediately.

Please consider our proposal favorably and respond with your answer at your earliest convenience. We'd love to establish a firm trading relation with you.

Sincerely,

Taylor Kennedy

Questions:

(1) What changes is Mr. Kennedy proposing to Mr. Henry Kingsbury?
(2) Why does Mr. Kennedy make the proposal?
(3) Does Mr. Kennedy expect total agreement from Mr. Henry?
(4) How long are the motor bikes warrantied according to the original offer from Mr. Henry?
(5) Which words in the letter have a similar meaning to the following?
    A. recommended   B. besides   C. consideration   D. willing

3. Fill in the blanks to complete the letter.

Dear Mr. Mark

Thank you for your (1)_____ (及时地回复和报盘) of June 6.

We are (2)_____ (对于医疗器材的质量和交货日期都很满意). Nevertheless, the present economic situation is quite difficult and we are forced to (3)_____ (降低成本). We expect (4)_____ (请求贵方能降价10%). In return, we will place orders up to US$10,000 with you this year.

Please let me know if the concession (5)_____ (能被满足).

Yours sincerely

Self-evaluation

1. Can you translate the following phrases into English?

(1) 还盘　　　　　(2) 让步　　　　　(3) 减价10%　　　　(4) 包装
(5) 礼品包装　　　(6) 行业折扣　　　(7) 现金折扣　　　　(8) 一周内交货
(9) 缩短交货日期　(10) 送货上门　　(11) 同意账期　　　　(12) 提供资信证明
(13) 底价　　　　(14) 拒绝还盘　　(15) 延长保修期　　　(16) 广告宣传费用
(17) 提交新的标书 (18) 大量订货　　(19) 经常订购　　　　(20) 扩大代理范围

2. Please translate the sentences into English.

(1) 虽然我们明白这款产品的保健作用，但是我方不确定顾客对这款高端产品会有什么反应。

(2) 如果同意我们赊购，我们就长期购买您的产品。

(3) 尽管我们很想让您成为我方的供货商，但是您上封信里的报价使得这根本不可能。

(4) 我们很有信心，辅以广告资助，您产品的销售将很快超出同类竞争品牌。

(5) 在这种情况下，我方要求您降价10%。

(6) 我们通常在收到发票7日内付清货款，因此希望得到1.5%的现金折扣。

(7) 如果在20%的行业折扣之外，你方再提供一个5%的数量折扣，我们就订购你家的产品。

(8) 如果价格能降20%，这笔生意就归您。

(9) 如果货物破损，保险公司拒赔，客户的损失您能承担的情况下，我们可以接受您用纸壳箱运输货物。

（10）我方对于顾客的反应尚无把握，想先试销 3 个月。

（11）如果能接受我们的要求，我们就大量订购。

（12）价格有竞争力的话，您的蔬菜和水果能很畅销。

（13）我们想尝试一下贵厂的新产品。不过，我们要求收到订单后 3 周内交货。

（14）我们检查了您的样品，对它的质量和款式都很满意。只是现金交单对我们的资金周转压力太大。

（15）您的产品质量达到了我方的要求，但是您的价格和其他供货商的价格差别巨大。

3. Please translate the sentences into Chinese.

(1) We agree with you that there is a growing demand for them in our country.

(2) If you could shorten the delivery from 6 weeks to 4 weeks from receipt of order, please let us know.

(3) If you can comply with our request to reduce the prices by 10%, we will send you our official orders for 3000 units.

(4) We found your price is 10% above the market price.

(5) Is there any wiggle room on that price?

(6) Please quote your shipment and insurance if you can shorten the delivery from 4 weeks to two weeks for the shipment of Tokyo, Japan.

(7) As a rule our suppliers allow us quarterly settlements.

(8) We mainly settle our accounts on a D/A basis with payment by 30-day B/E.

(9) If the concessions we asked for can be met, we will order on a regular basis.

(10) As we work on a fast turnover, small profit margin basis we expect a 30% trade discount.

(11) We counter-offer as follows, subject to your confirmation reaching us before the end of the May: 600 pieces pure cotton shirts at US$37 per piece CIF Boston, others terms as per your email of March 1.

(12) However, we would only consider placing an order if it was on the usual basis of sale or return. If this is acceptable, we will send you a firm order.

(13) Door-to-door delivery is a firm condition of our order. If you can offer it, we would buy from you.

(14) We expect an annual US$ 6000 in advertising allowances. With it, we are sure that your machines will become a market-leader.

(15) This is the best price we can offer. Our high quality justifies the quotation. You will find it profitable to buy from us.

Did you make any grammer mistake?
Did you make any spelling mistake?
Did you apply the correct business words and adopt proper patterns in your sentences?

4. Can you write back to a supplier, negotiating a price deduction according to the details given below?

(1) with reference to	(2) ask for a discount	(3) place orders
(4) increase sale	(5) mutual benefit	(6) establish long term relationship

Did you acknowledge receipt of the offer from the seller?
Did you mention the change(s) you would like to make to the business terms offered?
Did you encourage further contact at the end of the counter-offer?

You can move on to Unit Six if you can complete the exercises satisfactorily.

Unit Six
Order

In business or commerce, an order is a stated intention, either spoken or written, to engage in a commercial transaction for specific products or services. From a buyer's point of view it expresses the intention to buy and is called a purchase order. A purchase order (PO) is like a reverse invoice, being issued by the individual or company making the purchase. The document represents the customer's intent to buy a clear quantity of items. Importantly, it explicitly states the agreed cost. Once a provider accepts a purchase order, a binding contract is formed between the buyer and the seller. The buyer commits to receive something from the seller and to pay for it, and the seller commits to supply the buyer with the goods or service asked for at the price agreed upon. Order can be sent by email, fax, or post.

A company's number one objective is to get orders, namely, to boost sales.

A purchase order is likely to include the following details:

- PO number - An essential detail, as the buyer will match this to their original purchase order when they receive an invoice with a delivery, cross referencing to see they have the right items, in the correct quantity, at the agreed price.
- Purchaser details - Including the name of a point of contact, the preferred shipping address, plus a telephone number and email contact.
- Supplier details - Including their name, address and contact number or email.
- Payment terms - The timeframe within which the invoice should be paid. Payment terms of 30 days after delivery are common.
- Shipping method - Whether by air, freight or regular post.
- Shipping date and term - The desired date of dispatch and how long delivery is likely to take.
- Item number (if applicable) - This may be a catalogue reference code.
- Description of goods or services
- Quantity (if applicable)
- Price per unit
- Total - Excluding appropriate taxes (e.g. Value Added Tax (VAT) in the UK).

- Appropriate taxes (if applicable) - e.g. VAT.
- Total net

A standard purchase order template looks something like this:

Purchase Order

Date:

PO number:

Purchaser:

Delivery address: address, telephone number and email address

Supplier: name, address, telephone number and email address

Shipping method	**Shipping date**	**Term**
air / freight / post	DD/MM/YYY	X days

Item number	**Description**	**Quantity**	**Price**	**Total**
B376	Grey cotton pillow cases	80	£6.30	£504
B629	White cotton bed covers	40	£26.80	£1072
			Sub-total	£1576
			VAT (20%)	£315.2
			Total net	£1387.2

Signature: **Date:**

---

or

Purchase Order

Serial:_____

Number:_____

Vendor's Name and Address _____

_____

Delivery Date: _____

Terms of Payment: _____
Delivery Point: _____
Order Date _____

Sign Date

Item No.	Specification	Unit	Quantity	Unit Price	Total Value

Amount in Words: _____
Currency: _____

Unit Objectives

After learning the unit, students should be able to:
1. **Understand business orders and their forms;**
2. **Know how to write covering letters;**
3. **Recognize and remember related expressions and sentence patterns and apply the above in related business activities;**
4. **Acknowledge an order;**
5. **Advise the buyer with an advice note that the order has been made up and shipment has been arranged;**
6. **Inform your buyers of delays in delivery;**
7. **Turn down orders properly.**

Structure & Content

❖ Covering Letter

A purchase order is likely to be accompanied by a covering letter, which gives the buyer the opportunity to make any necessary points and confirm the business terms and discount that have been agreed. It may also include the details of order, quantity, color, and kind of product, the mode of payment and date(s) of shipment etc. It helps avoid misunderstandings and allows both parties to have a copy of the details of the transaction. It can also serve as a stand-alone form of communication.

❖ Confirmation of Business Terms

It is good practice to confirm the business terms and conditions of the sale in the covering letter. That way there can be no misunderstandings or changes in the terms agreed upon.

❖ Acknowledgement of an Order

The supplier is expected to thank the customer for placing an order with him and make it clear in the beginning whether the needs of the buyer can be satisfied or not. It can be irritating to read a long letter and only find the need cannot be met.

❖ Acceptance of an Order

When the supplier receives and acts on the purchase order request, they're formally accepting its terms and creating a legal agreement between the two parties. The order is "in progress" until the agreed work is completed or the items sent and the order fulfilled. The seller will generate an invoice that records the details on the buyer's purchase order — what has been provided, in what quantity, how much it will cost and when payment is expected.

❖ Advice Note

When the supplier has made up the order and arranged shipment, the customer is informed by means of an advice note.

❖ Advice of Delays in Delivery

If the goods ordered cannot be delivered within the time specified, held up either before or after they are dispatched, the seller should keep the customer informed, explaining what has happened, how it happened, and what are being done to put things right. The sooner the customer is informed, the better he can be prepared for the delay, and the sooner he can take action.

❖ Decline of an Order

The seller may decline an order for several reasons: he may not have the goods in stock, the terms are not favorable, the buyer may have a bad reputation in settling his account promptly or offering poor after-sale services, etc. When turning down an order, the seller must be polite.

Rejection letters should be short and polite. You are expected to first of all thank the customers for his or her interest in your product, state your decision together with reasons, and finally wrap up the letter with a brief note of thanks, a courteous salutation, and a signature.

Example One Placing an order

Dear Mr. Montreal,

Please find the attached order for the following items:

30 V-necked sweaters, Catalogue number V372, $16.00/ Piece.
30 crew-necked pullovers, Catalogue number T891, $22.00/ Piece.

Payment will be made within 30 days from the date of the invoice.

We look forward to hearing from you soon.

Thank you.

Yours sincerely,

Ms. Valve Long

Making it clear an order is placed
Details of the order

Confirming payment terms

Encouraging further contacts

Example Two Acknowledging receipt of an order

Dear Anna,

Thank you for your order for 30 garden umbrellas, Catalogue T4736, and for your prompt online payment. Your order will be shipped within three to five business days. We will keep you informed of its latest development.

We are glad you chose our company for garden umbrellas. As our well-illustrated brochures state, we offer a large variety of umbrellas which are high in quality, beautiful in design and competitive in price. And our umbrellas can be made as per the specific requirements of our clients.

We have attached our latest spring catalogue, which can give you a rough idea of the new lines we are producing for the coming season. And you can visit our website for more detailed information. Please note that a 5% loyalty discount is offered to regular customers.

Acknowledging receipt of the order
Advising shipment

Stressing selling points

Offering more information of products

Thank you for shopping with us. Sincerely yours, Ms. Judy Church	Thanking the customer for the business

Example Three Turning down an order

Dear Mr. Zhang,	
I was very glad to receive your purchase order for 3 of our Snow Wolf down-filled coats.	Acknowledging receipt of the order
I must say that you have made a wise and good choice regarding to the down-filled coats. However, as a manufacturer, we only deal with wholesalers, not individual customers. And to insure the local representation, its consistency, and the uniformity of the service, we only market our goods through appointed agents.	Buffering the refusal Turning down the order diplomatically
Please take note of the name and address of the local dealer in your area: *Dashang Group, 11 Qingniwa, Dalian, Liaoning* Please contact Dashang, who carries a full range of our products.	Referring the customer to those who can help
Thank you for your business. Yours sincerely, Brain Fisher	End the refusal with a positive note

Expressions to Learn and Remember

Terms to remember

Order	place an order for; provisional order; trail order; official order; purchase order; acknowledge an order; decline an order
Business terms	terms of payment; credit facilities; open account terms; on approval; discounts
Package	be packed in crates
Shipment	make shipment; advice shipment
Dispatch	be ready for dispatch; dispatch the goods
Delivery	prompt delivery; late delivery; guarantee delivery

Sentence Patterns for application

Placing an order

1. Please find enclosed our order (No. K416) for 30 kits of the coffee table assemblies.
2. The enclosed order (No. n52) is for 50 packets of "Golden Leaf" cigarettes.
3. Enclosed you will find our order (No. A089) for 300 of your "Little Swan" washing machines.
4. I would like to place a trial order for the bamboo mattresses we discussed at the trade show last month.
5. Thank you for your reply of 23 August regarding our email about the leather couches. Enclosed you will find our official order (No. A 561) for 10 of the leather couches, Cat. CSC137.
6. As we find your prices competitive and terms of payment acceptable, we are placing an order for 1500 water-proof drills.

Confirming business terms

1. We would like to thank you for the 30% trade discount and 10% quantity discount you allowed us.
2. We will take advantage of the 3% cash discounts you offered for payment made within one week.

3. We are pleased with the 25% trade discount and delivery date you promised and have decided to place a trial order with you for 200 sets of your tableware.
4. Delivery before the end of April is a firm condition of this order, and we reserve the right to refuse goods delivered after that time.
5. Please confirm that you can deliver the order within one week of receipt of the parcel, as it is needed urgently.
6. In spite of our anticipation of a higher trade discount than 22%, we will place an initial order and hope that the discount can be reviewed in the future.

Packaging instructions

1. The consignment of 50 sets of crockery should be packed in ten crates, five sets per crate, with each piece individually wrapped.
2. The packages/crates should be lined inside and marked outside with their names, the words "fragile", "crockery" , "This side up" and "numbered 1~10".
3. Each piece of crockery is to be wrapped in thick paper, ten pieces in a wooden crate/case, marked with ◊ and destination and numbered 1~6.
4. The dinner sets have been put into wooden crates, which are clearly marked with your castle logo for easy identification.

Stressing delivery

1. Prompt delivery is to be guaranteed.
2. Please deliver the goods before Friday in time for our Saturday promotion.
3. Delivery by the end of May is a firm condition of this order and we reserve the right to refuse late deliveries.
4. It is essential that the furniture be delivered by November for the Black Friday Sale.
5. These fabrics are for a priority client who is planning for a wedding and we would appreciate your prompt delivery.

Advising dispatch

1. Your order has been fulfilled and shipment will be made within 48 hours.
2. The carpets you ordered are already on board "Orient Pearl", sailing from Shanghai on 6 May and arriving Boston 6 June.

3. We are pleased to advise you that the flowers you ordered will be on flight CA 8097, leaving Kunming at 8:50, 9 August, arriving Tokyo at 16:00 9 August.

4. The cupboards will be sent express rail-freight and can be collected in Dalian Railway Station after 3pm, 2 December. Attached you will find consignment note No. 11206, which should be presented on collection.

Informing delays in delivery

1. I am sorry to tell you that there will be a three-week delay in delivery. This is due to a fire which has destroyed most of the stock in the warehouse of our paper mill.

2. Your consignment of cotton quilts will not reach you as scheduled due to a local dispute on the cargo vessel on which they are loaded. I am sorry for the delay and shall keep you informed of the latest development.

3. We regret to inform you that there will be a delay in getting your consignment to you, as you may be aware, a snow storm has stopped all the traffic in the Northeast. I apologize for this delay, which is due to circumstances beyond our control.

4. The delay is caused by a cut in supplies from US, where the government has put an embargo on chips to be exported to China. We are now contacting possible suppliers who may help us. If you wish to cancel your order, please let us know as soon as possible.

5. Four weeks ago when you placed the order with us, we had expected to be able to complete the order well within the delivery date which was 18 September, but since then we have heard that our main supplier has gone bankrupt.

Making specific requirements

1. Your prompt execution of our order would be appreciated.

2. Please acknowledge the receipt of our order and fax your invoice for prepayment.

3. We are looking forward to your confirmation of the order.

4. The machines must be well greased with all movable parts secured before being loaded.

Samples for Comprehension

❖ Sample One Writing to Confirm Telephone Order

Dear Mr. Kingsbury,

Thank you for talking with me today about your newly-developed interactive teaching tools. I am writing to confirm our telephone order for 200 copies of the Kindergarten Math Fun you recommended.

I understand that the book is $50 each and that you offer us a 10% quantity discount. As we will make our own arrangement to pick up the books from your warehouse, no delivery charges will be added to the total price of the $900.

As we discussed, we will have a check ready when we pick up the books on August 15.

Thank you again.

Sincerely yours,

Mary Moor

❖ Sample Two Confirming Telephone Conversation

Dear Mr. Lee,

This letter is a confirmation of our recent telephone conversation where you agreed to purchase the following items from our company. These are the details:

30 V-necked sweaters, Catalogue number V372, $16.00/Piece.

30 turtle-necked pullovers, Catalogue number T891, $22.00/Piece.

When we receive your official order, this will mean that you agree to the printed terms and conditions for the merchandise which accompanies the letter. It also means that you agree to the payment terms which are 30 days from the date of the invoice.

Please sign a copy of this letter and return it to me with your official order. Once we have received them, we will deliver the items to you according to the delivery schedule agreed upon.

We look forward to hearing from you soon.

Thank you.

Yours sincerely,

Ms. Valve Long

❖ Sample Three Placing an Order

Dear Mr. Baker,

We would like to purchase 10 chest drawers, 10 oak breakfast tables, 40 wooden chairs, and 10 stainless sinks.

Please charge this purchase to the preexisting account that we have with you, business account #3308395.

We hope to receive this order no later than Friday, 5 November, 2021. Attached to the email please find our packaging instructions, preferred shipping method and receiving addresses.

Please confirm that you receive our order by calling us at 9307866 any time during business hours, Monday to Friday.

Sincerely yours,

Ian Stone

❖ Sample Four Advising Dispatch of Goods

Dear Mr. Cross,

We are glad to tell you that the 300 straw hats you ordered last week has been picked up by UPS, who promises us the goods will be delivered to you in 15 business days.

Meanwhile, our bank has forwarded the relevant documents and sight draft for $1500 which includes the agreed trade, to Bank of America, Madison.

We are sure you will be pleased with the consignment and look forward to your future orders.

Best regards,

Gary Davos

Tasks to Fulfill

scan for the keys

1. Can you answer the questions?

(1) What is a covering letter?
(2) What is included in a covering letter?
(3) What sort of information can be found in a PO?
(4) When is an order likely to be declined?

2. Read and answer the following questions.

Dear Ms. Corleone,

Thank you for your prompt reply.

We are happy with your quality and quotation, and are enclosing an order for 600 pcs. Notebooks, catalogue No. 5109.

Thank you for the 30% trade discount and the 2% cash discount you offered us for payment made within 7 days of receipt of the consignment.

We would appreciate it if the order can be delivered early next month in time for our autumn semester.

Enclosed you will find a check in the sum of $1000 as down payment on the notebooks. The remaining will be paid in cash upon delivery.

Sincerely yours,

Ms. Eliza Bungan
Financial Accountant

Questions:

(1) What is enclosed in the letter?
(2) Does the supplier offer any discount?
(3) How can Eliza enjoy an additional 2% discount besides the 30% trade discount?
(4) When is the consignment needed?
(5) Which words in the letter have a similar meaning to the following?
    A. timely   B. fall   C. rest   D. paid

3. Fill in the blanks to complete the letter.

Dear Ms. Brennan,

(1)_____（关于）your quotation dated 12th July 2021, we (2)_____（订购 6000 本）exercise books of 200 pages each branded with our school logo.

We would appreciate it if (3)_____（交货）by 1st August 2021 so that we can make the proper arrangements when school resumes in September. Our address is 121 Beacon Street, Boston.

(4)_____（货到付现金）.

Please (5)_____（确认收到并接受我方订单）by email before 5 June.

If we don't receive the consignment by the 1st of August 2021, we will cancel the order and get it fulfilled by other suppliers. Please also provide tracking information to our email address for follow up at Brainschool@yahoo.com.

Thank you.

Sincerely yours

Brain Siemen
President

Self-evaluation

1. Can you translate the following phrases into English?

(1) 订单　　　　　　(2) 附函　　　　　　(3) 账单　　　　　　(4) 包装指令
(5) 确认交易条款　　(6) 完成订单　　　　(7) 经常订购　　　　(8) 取消订单
(9) 拒绝订单　　　　(10) 延迟交货　　　　(11) 按时交货　　　　(12) 商业单证
(13) 发货通知　　　　(14) 延误　　　　　　(15) 禁运　　　　　　(16) 装船
(17) 木条箱　　　　　(18) 无法控制的原因　(19) 确认收到订单　　(20) 货源中断

2. Please translate the sentences into English.

(1) 信中附有订单一份，号码为 A46，订购贵厂 60 套茶几，请两周内送达。

(2) 我方打算试购贵方正在以成本价出售的皮毛大衣，并且按照我们上周电话里商定的那样用信用证支付货款。

(3) 按照我们双方的协定，付款方式为承兑交单，您开具以我方为付款人的 30 天汇票一张，单证交付中国银行大连分行。

(4) 您提供的 25% 的折扣低于我方的预期，但是我们还是决定先从您这里购买一批货物，希望您将来能重新考虑给我们的折扣。

(5) 我们急需这批货，请空运以确保按时到达。

(6) 我们建议陆运货物，以免不断的装卸对这批易碎货物造成损伤。

(7) 您订购的电脑已经送往神户码头，正等待装上"东方明珠"轮船，该船 7 月 26 号驶往天津，预计 30 号抵达。

(8) 对不起您的货物还没到，经查询，这批货物目前停留在汉堡港，那里的工人在罢工，造成了这次延误。很遗憾发生了这件我们无法控制的情况，给您造成了不便我们在此向您道歉。

(9) 对不起，您要的空调没货了，下一批要 3 周才来货。我们到货了就通知您。

(10) 对不起，您订购的"蓝天牌"电视机无法按时交货了，因为，您也许听说了，上周日本发生了强烈地震，很多工厂都被震毁了。

(11) 谢谢您订购我们的产品，但是目前需求量大，而我们库存有限，只能轮流供货。无法在您限定的时间内完成您的订单。

(12) 工厂现在正在往普兰店搬迁，无法给您一个确切的交货日期，很抱歉不能给您供货。

(13) 我们是薄利多销，您要的折扣太大，我们不赚钱。

(14) 谢谢您订购我们的货物。我们正在给您备货，预计本周末之前备齐并发货。我们将随时通知您最新的进展。

(15) 我们同意这批货您给我们 15% 的折扣，并要求我们用即期汇票现金交单的方式支付货款。但是我们希望以后再购买时您能修改这些条件。

3. Please translate the sentences into Chinese.

(1) Please find enclosed our order Number OG186119 for 300 bottles of your extra virgin olive oils.

(2) I would like to place a trial order for the bamboo mattresses we discussed at the trade show last month.

(3) As we find your prices competitive and terms of payment acceptable, we are placing an order for 1500 water-proof drills.

(4) We are pleased with the 25% trade discount and delivery date you promised and have decided to place a trial order with you for 200 sets of your tableware.

(5) Please confirm that you can deliver the order within one week of receipt of the parcel, as it is needed urgently.

(6) Each piece of crockery is to be wrapped in thick paper, ten pieces in a wooden crate, marked with destination and numbered 1~6.
(7) Thank you for the above order which we are now making up. We will advise you about shipment in the next few days.
(8) Please deliver the goods before Friday in time for our Saturday promotion.
(9) We are pleased to advise you that the flowers you ordered will be on flight CA 8097, leaving Kunming at 8:50, 9 August, arriving Tokyo at 16:00, 9 August.
(10) I am sorry to tell you that there will be a three-week delay in delivery. This is due to a fire which has destroyed most of the stock in the warehouse of our paper mill.
(11) This delay is caused by a cut in supplies due to extreme weather.
(12) If you wish to cancel your order, please let us know as soon as possible.
(13) Thank you for your order No. LH1106 which we received today. Unfortunately, we cannot offer the 25% trade discount you asked for.
(14) I apologize for this delay, which is due to circumstances beyond our control.
(15) This is the best price we can offer, even on large orders, as our prices are extremely competitive.

Did you make any grammar mistake?
Did you make any spelling mistake?
Did you apply the correct words and patterns in your sentences?

4. You have decided to place an order with a Canadian supplier and plan to write a letter accompanying the order based on the details given below.

> (1) An order for 120 down-filled coats
> (2) Acknowledgement of receipt of the order expected
> (3) Detailed information including patterns, colors, and sizes
> (4) 18% trade discount, 5% quantity discount
> (5) Delivery within 4 weeks from receipt of order
> (6) Long term business relationship expected
> (7) Payment to be made by letter of credit

Did you mention an order is attached?
Did you make it clear that acknowledgement of receipt of the order is expected?
Did you confirm the business terms reached?
Did you express your wish for further business cooperation in the future?

You can move on to Unit Seven if you can complete the exercises satisfactorily.

Unit Seven

Payment

A payment is a transfer of funds or monetary value. A payment transaction involves two end parties: On one side, the debtor or payer who sends the funds and on the other side, the creditor or payee who receives the funds. An end party can be the sender or receiver of payment. It is a party involved in any side of a payment transaction. Payments are generally made in exchange for the provision of goods, services between end parties, or to meet legal obligations.

Payment instruments can be divided in two categories: cash payment instruments and non-cash payment instruments. Cash is money in the physical form of currency, such as banknotes and coins. Non-cash payment instruments are multiple: Checks, Cards, Credit Transfers, Direct Debits, E-Money, etc.

In addition, Credit Note or Debit Note is usually used to adjust or rectify errors made in a sales invoice which has already been processed and sent to a customer.

A Credit Note is a refund to a customer's account. It may be issued in the case of damaged goods, errors or allowances.

A debit note is a charge to a customer's account. It is generally given by a customer to a supplier, indicating that an account has been debited.

If you have already sent an invoice to a customer but now need to provide a credit note or a debit note for that invoice, you would send them a Credit Note or Debit Note. For example, you issued an invoice for an item for $1100 when the correct price of the item should have been $1010 or $1110 instead. Therefore you need to issue a Credit Note to give a credit of $90 or a debit note to give a debit of $10 to your customer for the amount over-billed or under-billed. Some other examples are listed below.

Faulty goods returned or goods rejected by customer.

Goods short or over-shipped: You invoiced a customer for 10 units of your product but only shipped 9 or 11 units to them by mistake. The customer then calls you to say that 9 units are okay and he does not want the shortfall item at the moment or they can accept the extra unit. Therefore you need to issue a Credit Note or a Debit Note to credit or debit your customer for the shortfall or over-landed quantity of 1 unit.

Product wrongly shipped: You wrongly invoiced and shipped Product A when the customer actually ordered Product B which may or may not be at a different price. To rectify this, you would then ship Product B together with a Credit Note for Product A and another invoice for Product B. This will restore the inventory and Accounts Receivable in your books while billing the customer for the correct item and amount. Meanwhile the customer returns the incorrect Product A.

To write-off customer short payments: You send an invoice for say $2010. The customer sends you a short payment of $2000 only. You do not wish to recover the shortfall amount but your books indicate that $10 is still owing on this invoice. You can then issue a credit note of $10 to write off the shortfall amount.

Getting paid in full and on time is the ultimate goal for each export sale. For exporters, any sale is a gift until payment is received. Therefore, exporters want to receive payment as soon as possible, preferably as soon as an order is placed or before the goods are sent to the importer. For importers, any payment is a donation until the goods are received. Therefore, importers want to receive the goods as soon as possible but to delay payment as long as possible, preferably until after the goods are resold to generate enough income to pay the exporter. Therefore, appropriate payment methods must be chosen carefully to minimize the payment risk while also accommodating the needs of the buyers.

There are plenty of international paying methods for importers and exporters across the globe. The main international payment methods used around the world today include: Cash in Advance, Letters of Credit, Documentary Collections, Open Account, and Consignment.

With cash-in-advance payment terms, an exporter can avoid credit risk because payment is received before the ownership of the goods is transferred. For international sales, wire transfers and credit cards are the most commonly used cash-in-advance options available to exporters.

Letters of credit (L/Cs) are one of the most secure instruments available to international traders. An L/C is a commitment by a bank on behalf of the buyer that payment will be made to the exporter, provided that the terms and conditions stated in the L/C have been met. The buyer establishes credit and pays his or her bank to render this service. An L/C is useful when reliable credit information about a foreign buyer is difficult to obtain, but the exporter is satisfied with the creditworthiness of the buyer's foreign bank. An L/C also protects the buyer since no payment obligation arises until the goods have been shipped as promised.

There are many different letters of credit including one called a standby L/C (payable when the beneficiary did not receive what was promised, more as insurance and less as a means of facilitating an exchange）．

Irrevocable letters of credit are commonly used in international trade. These stipulate that no amendments or cancellations can occur without the consent of all parties involved.

Example One Application for irrevocable standby letter of credit

---

APPLICATION FOR IRREVOCABLE STANDBY LETTER OF CREDIT

To _____ Bank

Please issue your irrevocable standby letter of credit in according with the following terms and conditions:

1. APPLICANT

2. ISSUSING BANK

3. BENEFICIARY

4. AMOUNT $_____ US Dollars

5. DATE and TIME EXPIRATION

6. PAYMENT INSTRUCTIONS
Payment shall be made at Beneficiary's request and upon its presentation of 1) a sight draft, 2) the original letter of credit, 3) copy of invoice, and 4) a statement purportedly signed by Beneficiary stating that Applicant has failed to fulfill its contractual obligation.
7. SPECIAL CONDITIONS

Dated as of the _____ day of _____

APPLICANT NAME
By:_____
APPLICANT NAME AND TITLE

Example Two Irrevocable standby letter of credit

IRREVOCABLE STANDBY LETTER OF CREDIT

Our Letter of Credit Number:

Date:

Beneficiary:

Applicant:

Gentlemen:

At the request of applicant, we hereby issue our irrevocable standby letter of credit number _____ which is available by payment against beneficiary's draft at sight, drawn on _____ Bank, at ADDRESS.

This credit is for an aggregate amount not to exceed a total of U.S. Dollar $ _____. Draft submitted must be accompanied by the following documents:

1. The original of this Letter of Credit.
2. A copy of the invoice unpaid by Applicant.
3. A sworn statement purported signed by Beneficiary certifying that Applicant has failed to fulfill its contractual obligations.

This letter of credit expires at the counters of _____ Bank at ADDRESS at _____ p.m.(CST) on DATE.

IRREVOCABLE STANDBY LETTER OF CREDIT

Page 2

We hereby agree to honor all drafts in compliance with the terms of and drawn under _____ Bank Irrevocable Standby Letter of Credit number _____ dated _____, on or before the expiration date.

In order to cancel this letter of credit prior to expiration, this letter of credit must be returned to us for cancellation with a statement purportedly signed by the beneficiary stating that: "This letter of credit is no longer required by us and is herewith returned to you for cancellation."

> This letter of credit is issued subject to and governed by the Laws of the State of Texas and the 1993 Revision of the Uniform Customs and Practice for Documentary Credits of the International Chambers of Commerce (Publication No.500) and in the event of any conflict, the Laws of Texas will preside.
>
> _____ Bank
>
> _____
> By: LENDER

A documentary collection (D/C) is a transaction whereby the exporter entrusts the collection of the payment for a sale to its bank (remitting bank 寄单行), which sends the documents that its buyer needs to the importer's bank (collecting bank 代收银行), with instructions to release the documents to the buyer for payment. Funds are received from the importer and remitted to the exporter through the banks involved in the collection in exchange for those documents. D/Cs involve using a draft that requires the importer to pay the face amount either at sight (document against payment) or on a specified date (document against acceptance). The collection letter gives instructions that specify the documents required for the transfer of title to the goods. Although banks do act as facilitators for their clients, D/Cs offer no verification process and limited recourse in the event of non-payment. D/Cs are generally less expensive than L/Cs.

An open account transaction is a sale where the goods are shipped and delivered before payment is due, which in international sales is typically in 30, 60 or 90 days. It is one of the most advantageous options to the importer in terms of cash flow and cost, but it is consequently one of the highest risk options for an exporter.

Consignment, a variation of open account in which payment is sent to the exporter only after the goods have been sold by the foreign distributor to the end customer, is based on a contractual arrangement in which the foreign distributor receives, manages, and sells the goods for the exporter who retains title to the goods until they are sold. Clearly, exporting on consignment is very risky as the exporter is not guaranteed any payment and its goods are in a foreign country in the hands of an independent distributor or agent. Consignment helps exporters become more competitive on the basis of better availability and faster delivery of goods. Selling on consignment can also help exporters reduce the direct costs of storing and managing inventory. The key to success in exporting on consignment is to partner with a reputable and trustworthy foreign distributor or a third-party logistics provider.

There is always a certain level of risk and trust involved. In large part, the amount of risk involved highly depends on the method of payment you use.

Unit Objectives

After learning the unit, students should be able to:
1. Understand various methods of payment and their process;
2. Recognize and remember related expressions and sentence patterns;
3. Apply the above in their trade practices related to payment.

Structure & Content

❖ Negotiating Payment

Negotiating better payment terms means you can keep more cash in your business and improve liquidity, so you'll be in a better place to pay bills and avoid having to go overdrawn or seek loans.

Do you allow open account terms? We can provide necessary references. As a rule, our suppliers allow us to settle by monthly statement and we can offer the usual references if necessary. We would like to point out that we usually settle our accounts on a D/A basis with payment by 30-day bill of exchange.

We would only consider placing an order if it was on the usual basis of sale or return. If this is acceptable, we will send you a firm order.

Would it be possible for you to supply us with a range on an approval basis to see if we can encourage a demand?

As we usually place large orders, we feel we are able to ask for better credit facilities from you.
We usually deal on payment by sight draft, cash against documents, and we do not offer credit facilities for initial orders.
Is Net 60 acceptable to you?

We usually accept payment by irrevocable L/C, payment against documents.

For large orders, we insist on payment by L/C.
As our products are competitively priced, it is uneconomical to allow any credit facilities.
As our business relations with you over the past two years have been entirely satisfactory, we are ready to change our transaction from payment on invoice to open account terms.

I regret that we cannot offer you credit for as long as three months, since this would be uneconomical for us. However, we are prepared to offer you settlement against monthly statements. Perhaps you would let me know if this is acceptable.

Though we do not usually offer credit facilities, we would be prepared to consider partial credit. In this case you would pay half your invoices on a cash basis, and the rest by 30-day bill of exchange. If this arrangement suits you, please contact us.

However we would be prepared to review this

once we establish a firm trading association with you.

With reference to your letter of 12 March, in which you asked for open account facilities, I will contact you as soon as the usual enquiries have been made.

Thank you for your letter in which you asked for credit facilities. At present we are writing to the referees you mentioned and will let you know as soon as we hear from them.

In reply to your email of 8 June, we will consider your request to pay by 30-day bill of exchange and will contact you by letter as soon as we have reached a decision.

Would you allow us a little time to consider the matter? I will be in touch with you again within the next couple of weeks.

We charge a returnable deposit of ¥1200. Payments should be made by credit card or bank draft in U.S. dollars.

❖ Granting Trade Credit

Trade credit has a significant impact on the financing of businesses. A trade credit is a business-to-business agreement which allows the exchange of goods and services without any immediate exchange of money. When the seller of goods or services allows the buyer to pay for the goods or services at a later scheduled date, the seller is said to grant credit facilities to the buyer. Providing credit allows convenience to the buyer, and thus leads to more orders. However, the seller may have default risk, as the buyer may be unable to pay off the required debt obligations. Credit facilities will only be granted by the seller if the buyer can satisfy one or more of these three requirements: reputation, long-term trading association, and references, which are often supplied when the buyer asks for credit facilities. Banks often act as referees.

As we have been trading for over a year, references will not be necessary. You may clear your accounts by Net 30.

I am glad to tell you that the open account terms you requested are acceptable. I would like to confirm that settlement will be made against monthly statements.

Due to the very good reputation of your company, we are willing to extend credit to you. You can pay by 60-day bill of exchange from your next order.
It is my pleasure to inform you that we have now received the necessary references and that you can settle your account on a documents against acceptance basis by 60-day B/E. Please make sure that the balance is paid in full when it's due, as late payment penalties may be added to your account.

❖ Refusing Credit

There are a number of factors that may result in a request for open account terms being refused. It might be uneconomical to offer credit facilities; some customers are considered bad risks; your own cash flow situation does not allow you to extend credit, or it might simply be that your company does not give credit. Whatever the reason, the reply must be worded carefully so as not to offend the customer.

Our company says it is expressly forbidden to grant credits to international buyers.

Once we have set up a stable business relation, we can allow our customers to buy on credit.
We do not offer open account terms, as our products are very competitive in price.

We are aware of your good reputation in your country, but credit facilities are offered to customers who can provide satisfactory references. We appreciate your request for buying on credit, but our cash flow does not allow us to do so. Once the situation improves, we will reconsider your request.

❖ Advising Payment

It is customary to advise the seller that payment is being made.
Enclosed you will find a check for the sum of $15,000 as payment on Proforma Invoice No. 55t2.

We have pleasure in enclosing our bank draft for $1200 in payment of your Invoice No. 3429 dated 12 May.

I have instructed my bank today to transfer $6478 to your account in payment of your 31 May statement.

We would like to inform you that we have arranged for a credit transfer through our bank, Bank of China, Dalian, for $2760 in settlement of my invoice of No. 2 order.

Our bank informs us that they now have the shipping documents, and will be transferring the proceeds of our letter of credit to your account.

You will be pleased to hear that we have accepted your bill and now have the documents.

We have pleasure in advising you that I have instructed my bank to credit £1,000 to your account with Bank of China, London.

❖ Acknowledging Payment

And the seller is expected to acknowledge receipt of payment from the buyer.

Thank you for paying so promptly, and we hope to hear from you again soon.
Thank you for sending your check for invoice No. 04209 so promptly.

I have received the €4376.00 you transferred to my account with Bank of China, Dalian.

We received the advice from our bank this morning that your transfer of €11068.00 for your October statement has been credited to our account. Thank you for your custom.

I am glad to tell you that we have received your bank draft for 84163.00 in settlement of invoice No.87079.

Our bank informed us today that you accepted our bill (No. 30078) and the documents have been transferred to you.

The Citi Bank in Huntsville told us that the proceeds of your letter of credit have been credited to our account.

Expressions to Learn and Remember

Terms to remember

Draft/bill of exchange	draw a draft on, pay by 30-day bill of exchange, settle our accounts on a D/A basis with payment by 30-day bill of exchange, deal on payment by sight draft, cash against documents
Bank draft	order a bank draft, pay by bank draft, a bank draft for four hundred thousand pounds
Check	accept a personal check, enclose a check, receive a check
Invoice	pay half your invoices on a cash basis
Proforma	We usually, and we do not offer credit facilities for initial orders
On approval basis	send goods to buyer on approval basis, buy on approval basis
Sale or Return	buy on Sale or Return, go into a Sale or Return arrangement, allow Sale or Return
Letter of credit	accept payment by irrevocable L/C, insist on payment by L/C, apply for an L/C, issue an L/C
Statement	pay by monthly statement, settle by quarterly statement, settlement against monthly statements

Sentence Patterns for Application

Asking for credit facilities

1. As a well-established company, our suppliers allow us to settle by quarterly statements.
2. We would place large orders if we can be allowed to pay by 30-day bill of exchange.
3. We would like to try a selection of your sweaters on an approval basis.
4. Do you accept Net 60?
5. What credit facilities do you offer?
6. Can we establish an open account, say a Net 30 account with your company?
7. Our international suppliers usually allow us to open account terms.

Granting credit facilities

1. With you good reputation, you can settle by monthly statements.
2. We are pleased to inform you that we accept payment by 30-day bill of exchange
3. As we have been trading for over a year, and you have always paid promptly, we are willing to allow you the credit facilities you asked for.
4. In view of our long-standing relationship, we are ready to change our transactions with you from payment on invoice to Net 30.
5. Though we always deal on a cash basis, we would be prepared to extend you the credit in view of our long time cooperation and your present situation.
6. If payment is made within 10 days, you can enjoy a 2% discount. If not, the full amount is due within 30 days.
7. We are pleased to inform you that the credit facilities you asked for are acceptable.

Suggesting compromises

1. We regret that we are unable to offer trade credit to initial buyers. However, we are willing to review this once we have established a firm trading relationship.
2. If you can increase your purchases by 50%, we would be willing to consider your request for credit arrangement.
3. We have to consider it as our sale final. You will find a $10 voucher enclosed with which you can use for your purchases of any item in our store.
4. You can pay half of the invoice by sight draft, and the remaining half by Net 30.
5. We cannot extend credit for as long as three months, but we are willing to accept D/A, with payment to be made by 30-day bill of exchange.
6. No credit facilities are allowed for the tables and chairs we are offering at cost price. You can pay by Net 30 with other stocks we have.
7. We are pleased to say that goods less than 1000 can be paid by monthly statement, however, should the amount exceed that figure, we insist on payment by letter of credit.

Denying request for credit facilities

1. We usually deal on payment by sight draft, cash against documents, and we do not offer credit facilities for initial orders.
2. It is the policy of the company that all payments for imports and exports must be made by irrevocable L/C.

3. We have considered your request for Net 60, and conclude that it would be uneconomical for us to allow credit on your present purchases.
4. A $1000-deposit is required for all orders, which is the company policy.
5. I am sorry we cannot put you on open account terms due to the very unstable exchange rate.
6. Our financial situation does not allow us to extend credit to customers.
7. We do need standard financial statement and bank references when considering credit requests from our customers. Please provide them, and we will hold the information in strictest confidence.

Samples for Comprehension

❖ Sample One Advising Payment Made in Full

Dear Wizard Window Washers,

Please find enclosed a check of $625, addressed to Mr. Jeremiah Bouchard.

This payment is the full amount owed for window cleaning services verbally agreed for the full year beginning July 3, 2011.

Please confirm in writing your receipt of this check and that our agreement has been met.

Furthermore I hereby confirm that I no longer require the window cleaning service, and any attempt to enter my property will be treated as trespassing.

Signed,

Karen Vargas

❖ Sample Two Granting Credit Facilities Asked for

Dear Mr. Cliff,

Thank you for your letter of April 6 in which you enquired about the credit facilities we can offer.

We are pleased to inform you that the credit facilities you asked for are acceptable, and for the good reputation your firm enjoys, there will be no need for us to contact any referees. Just to confirm what has been agreed between us, settlement will be made against monthly statements.

We look forward to receiving your next order.

Yours sincerely,

Ms Crane

❖ Sample Three Asking Payment by Monthly Settlement

Dear Mr. Merton,

Thank you for your catalogue and letter of March 8 which we received this morning. As there was no indication of your credit terms, I'd like to know if you would allow us to settle on a monthly statement basis.

You probably know that we are a well-established firm and we can certainly pay on the due dates, but if you would like confirmation covering our credit-worthiness then please contact any of the following who will act as our referees.

Red Star Plastics, Dalian,

Bank of China, Dalian Branch

Please follow up the references we have submitted. We hope you can consider our request favorably and look forward to your reply.

Yours sincerely,

Larry King

❖ Sample Four Asking for Changing to New Payment Term

Dear Mr. Brown,

I am writing to ask if it would be possible for us to have credit facilities in the form of payment by 60-day bill of exchange, documents against acceptance.

During the past two years of our transactions, we have always paid by confirmed, irrevocable letter of credit, which has indeed cost us a great deal. From the moment to open credit till the time our buyers pay us, the tie-up of our funds lasts about four months.

We feel you know us well enough to allow us to settle future accounts by 60-day bill of exchange, documents against payment.

If the credit facilities asked for can be granted, we'll send you our next order immediately.

Sincerely yours,

Thomas Church

❖ Sample Five Refusing to Grant Credit Facilities

Dear Mr. Brown,

Thank you for your letter of November 3 in which you asked to be put on open account terms.

We appreciate that you have placed a number of orders with us in the past several months and we are sure your company enjoys a very good reputation in your country. Nevertheless, it is our policy that credit facilities are allowed to customers who have traded with us for over three years. We really are sorry that we cannot be more helpful in this case.

Right now we would be happy to continue serving you on a cash basis.

Sincerely yours,

Mr. David Bishop

❖ Sample Six Asking to Buy on Credit

Dear Mr. J. Trump,

We are a fast-developing motor manufacturer and our car and truck business is growing so fast. We would like to open a credit account with a reputable company such as yours who can meet our large and frequent orders. It will be convenient and practical if we purchase on credit.

You may check our credit record, and you will see that we have a clean one. I believe that a $5000 credit line is acceptable for both of our companies. Attached is a completed credit application forward.

I hope to hear from you soon.

Sincerely yours,

Mr. Donald Roosevelt

Tasks to Fulfill

scan for the keys

1. Can you answer the questions?
(1) What are the main payment instruments and payment methods?
(2) Why do trading parties negotiate better payment terms?
(3) What are the factors a seller considers when granting credit requests?
(4) Why do sellers refuse credit request?

2. Read and answer the following questions.

Dear Robert,

Thank you for your order for 20 of our dressing tables. It is being handled now and will be dispatched within this week. Once we get all the shipping documents, we will forward them to your bank as usual.

With regard to your request for Net 45, I feel there would be more advantage for you in claiming the 2% cash discounts offered for payment made within seven days of receipt of invoice. Nevertheless, I am willing to allow you the credit you asked for. You can have 45 days from the invoice date to settle the account, without the 2% discount for early payment.

We look forward to hearing from you soon.

Yours sincerely,

Paul Gary

Questions:
(1) What is Mr. Gary doing concerning Mr. Robert's order?
(2) What request has Mr. Robert made about settlement of account?
(3) How has Mr. Robert been paying for goods up to now?
(4) With the new payment arrangement, when is Mr. Robert expected to settle his account?
(5) Which words in the letter have a similar meaning to the following?
    A. processed   B. sent   C. taking   D. ready

3. Fill in the blanks to complete the letter.

Dear Mr. Smith,

I am writing to request (1)_____ (改变付款方式). We have been (2)_____ (现金交易) for more than three months. As we are going to (3)_____ (增加购买量) and place large orders with you, we are requesting that you can allow us (4)_____ (收到发票 60 日内结算货款). With this arrangement, your sales will increase and our cash flow will improve.

Because of the large business volume, I believe it will be worthwhile for you to grant us the credit facilities. And we can (5)_____ (如果需要，可以提供资信证明).

Please consider our request favorably.

We look forward to hearing from you soon.

Sincerely yours,

Bernin Smith
Sales Manager

Self-evaluation

1. Can you translate the phrases into English?

(1) 支票　　　　　　(2) 汇票　　　　　　(3) 银行汇票　　　　(4) 见票后 30 天付款
(5) 货到付款　　　　(6) 跟单信用证　　　(7) 备用信用证　　　(8) 退款单 / 索款单
(9) 预交款　　　　　(10) 现金付款　　　　(11) 资信证明　　　　(12) 电汇
(13) 记账　　　　　　(14) 银行转账　　　　(15) 发货前　　　　　(16) 提交银行
(17) 申请开信用证　　(18) 通知付款　　　　(19) 告知对方已收到货款　(20) 信用证收益

2. Please translate the sentences into English.

(1) 通常供货商同意我们按月结算，如果需要，我们可以提供资信证明材料。

(2) 因为这是一款新产品，我们只能在贵厂同意我们无法销售可退货的情况下才能下订单。

(3) 您可以在 7 日内付款以享受 2% 的折扣。

(4) 我们通常的付款方式是承兑交单，30 天远期汇票。

（5）我们订货量很大，觉得可以申请更优惠的信用便利。

（6）只有和我们交易过一年以上的客户才能赊欠。

（7）我们通常是即期汇票，现金交单，而且对于新用户，概不赊欠。

（8）公司要求所有的进出口贸易必须用信用证结算。

（9）由于您一直按时结算货款，我们愿意将您的支付方式从见票即付变更至见票后60天付款。

（10）信中附有2500美元的支票一张，支付5512号形式发票的货款。

（11）很高兴在信中附上1200美元的银行汇票一张，支付5月15日的3429号发票。

（12）已通知我方银行今日转账至贵方账户2100美元，支付您5月31日的账单。转账成功后请告知为盼。

（13）很高兴告诉您我们已经承兑了您的汇票，并得到了所有的货运单据。

（14）银行今天通知我们说他们已经得到了货运单据，将把信用证的款额转入你的账户。

（15）中国银行大连分行今天告诉我们您信用证的款项已经转入我方账户。谢谢您及时结账。盼望不久得到您的消息。

3. Please translate the sentences into Chinese.

(1) We believe we have established our reliability with you over the past six months and would now like to settle accounts on a quarterly basis.

(2) We have been dealing with you for more than a year, and we have always settled promptly. Can you allow us to pay by 60-day bill of exchange now?

(3) I am sorry we cannot put you on open account terms due to the very unstable exchange rate.

(4) We have considered your request for Net 60, and conclude that it would be uneconomical for us to allow credit on your present purchases.

(5) If you can increase your purchases by 50%, we would be willing to consider your request for credit arrangement.

(6) We regret that we are unable to offer trade credit to initial buyers. However, we are willing to review this once we have established a firm trading relation.

(7) As we have been trading for over a year, references will not be necessary.

(8) You may clear your accounts by 60-day bill of exchange from your next order.

(9) We are pleased to inform you that the credit facilities you asked for are acceptable.

(10) Payment should reach our bank no later than 30 days from the invoice date.

(11) If payment is made within 10 days, you can enjoy a 2% discount. If not, the full amount is due within 30 days.

(12) Though we always deal on a cash basis, we would be prepared to extend you the credit in

view of our long time cooperation and your present situation.
(13) The $6000 as a deposit for your order No. 7078 has been transferred to our account at Standard Bank, Madison.
(14) With reference to the money transfer that you made this morning against the purchase of our sports shoes, I hereby acknowledge and confirm that I received the amount of $3000.
(15) We have received $6104 from you on 16 April as payment for the order you placed with us on 20 March.

Did you make any grammar mistake?
Did you make any spelling mistake?
Did you apply the correct business words and adopt proper patterns in your sentences?

4. Can you write to ask your supplier to allow you to open account term with the details given below?

| (1) retailer of air-conditioner | (2) first-class after-sale service | (3) settle promptly |
| (4) references | (5) place large orders | |

Did you introduce who you are and why you are writing to the supplier?
Did you mention that you are trustworthy?
Did you encourage the receiver to consider your request favorably by stating certain business terms?

You can move on to Unit Eight if you can complete the exercises satisfactorily.

Unit Eight
Requests for Payment & Replies

In international trade, problems involving bad debts are more easily avoided than rectified after they occur. When these problems do occur in international trade, obtaining payment can be both difficult and expensive. Even when the exporter has insurance to cover commercial credit risks, a default by a buyer still requires the time, effort, and cost of the exporter to collect a payment. The exporter must exercise normal business prudence in exporting and exhaust all reasonable means of obtaining payment before an insurance claim is honored. Even then there is often a significant delay before the insurance payment is made.

The best solution to a payment problem is to negotiate directly with the customer. If negotiations fail and the sum involved is large enough to warrant the effort, obtain the assistance of your bank, legal counsel, and other qualified experts. If both parties can agree to take their dispute to an arbitration agency, this step is faster and less costly than legal action.

When an account is past due, usually the seller will send out to the non-paying customer the first request for payment. When the customer offers neither payment nor explanation after two weeks, the second request will be sent. After you have demanded multiple times for payment in vain, you will send the final demand. You will be notifying the customer that if payment is not made within a certain time, you will be forced to refer the account to a collection agency or hand over the matter to a solicitor. Although it is not mandatory to let the customer know that the account has gone into collections or become a legal issue, it can help to keep the relationship in good standing and make a smooth transition. The final demand will also serve as proof of the multiple times the customer was contacted, the invoice in question and the amount that is due.

Unit Objectives

After learning the unit, students should be able to:
1. Understand structure and content of requests for payments & replies;
2. Recognize and remember related expressions and sentence patterns;
3. Apply the above in their business enquiries.

Structure & Content

When requesting for payment, bear in mind the three golden Ps:

Professional — go straight to the point, don't waste time, and be firm when discussing overdue payments.
Polite — do not get emotional, or accuse the client.
Persistent — continue reminding your client in a calm manner.

Written requests for payment, or collection letters, are usually written in a series, with the first request being just a simple reminder and the tone changing to a more direct and demanding one with successive letters. They are usually closed on a positive note.

❖ First Request for Payment & Reply

Since this is only the first letter, it is important to keep the tone friendly, informative and professional. Never immediately assume your customer has no intention of paying the account if the balance is overdue. There are many reasons why the customer has not paid on time, such as never receiving the invoice or overlooking the account. It is also possible that they have transferred the money to your account but your bank failed to inform you of the transfer. Therefore, a first request should take the form of a polite enquiry. Make sure you remain polite and professional.

Your request for overdue payment should contain the following information:

Days past due
Amount due
Instructions (what you would like them to do next)

Example One First request for payment

> Dear Mr. Davis:
>
> Outstanding Invoice #428
>
> Our records show that you have an outstanding balance dating back to May 7, 2020. The invoice was for $1,043.00 and we have not received the payment. Please find a copy of the invoice enclosed.
>
> If this amount has already been paid, please disregard this notice. Otherwise, please forward us the amount owed in full by the end of May, 2020. As our contract indicates, we begin charging 5% interest for any outstanding balances after 30 days.
>
> Thank you in advance for your cooperation. We hope to continue doing business with you in the future.
>
> Sincerely,
>
> Bozeman
> Accountant
>
> Enclosure: Invoice #223

Example Two Reply

Dear Mr. Bozeman,

Upon receiving your email which indicated that I had an outstanding balance with you in the amount of $1043.00, I consulted my bank, Nippon Bank, Kobe, and was told that the above amount has been transferred to your account on May 6.

You should have received my full payment prior to writing the email and I am, therefore, somewhat concerned.

Could you please check with your bank and find out if the fund has been deposited to your account?

Yours sincerely,

Toshiba

Example Three Reply

Dear Mr. Toshiba,

Thank you for helping us to locate your payment of May 6.

We apologize for this error and for the overdue notices we sent to you due to oversight on our part. We will do our best to avoid such a repetition in the future.

We appreciate your patronage and are sorry for the inconvenience caused.

Yours very sincerely,

Bozeman

❖ Second Request for Payment

If a customer intends to pay, they usually answer a first request immediately, offering an apology for having overlooked the account, or an explanation. But if they acknowledge your request but still do not pay, or do not answer at all, then you will have to make a second request. Though the tone of the second request becomes assertive with the first one gone ignored, you still need to remain friendly towards to customer.

In your second request, you should include the following information:

- Mention of your first request for overdue payment
- Original payment due date
- Days past due
- Invoice number and amount
- Instruction on what they should do next
- Offer help to work on the payment terms
- Hint at the impact non-payment could have on their credit terms/ratings

Example Four Request for payment

Dear Mr. Terrell,

I am contacting you again concerning your outstanding March statement, the balance of which is now three weeks overdue. Since I wrote to you on April 12, I have neither received your remittance nor any explanation as to why the balance of €6,000.00 has not been cleared. Please be reminded that there is a late fee for all statements after 30 days. Please would you either reply with an explanation or credit €6,000.00 to our account to clear the account within the next seven days?

> *I was wondering if any problems have arisen which I might be able to help you with. Please let me know if I can be of assistance.*
>
> *Thank you.*
>
> *John Smith*
> Credit Controller
>
> Encl.

Example Five Advice of payment

> Dear Mr. John Smith,
>
> You will receive €6,000.00, our full payment, for our March statement via bank transfer within 3 business days.
>
> I am sorry for the delay and the inconvenience this has caused you. An industrial dispute broke out in our factory two weeks ago and brought our production and office work to a sudden standstill, and that is why you got neither payment nor response from us. Now that the dispute is over and we are back to normal, there will be no late payments in the future.
>
> As you know, we have always been prompt in settling our accounts. This is an unfortunate exception.
>
> I apologize again for the inconvenience.
> Thank you for your patience.
> Yours very sincerely,
>
> *Louise Florica*

❖ Third or Final Request for Payment

Although the third request for payment can be quite frustrating, it is important to continue to remain restrained and professional. When no amount of persistence, emails, or phone calls can get your clients to clear the account with you, you may have to turn to a collection agent who can collect overdue payments for you at a percentage of the account receivable or hire an attorney to take legal actions against the clients or their company.

In the third or final request, simply state the facts and what the impending consequences will be. Inform the customer that if they do not pay immediately, you will be forced to refer their account to a collection agency or take legal actions to recover the debt, if you really intend to do so.

The third collection letter should include the following information:
- Mention of all previous attempts to collect
- Invoice number and amount
- Original invoice due date
- Current days past due
- Instructions on what they should do next
- A warning of the impending consequences
- Your contact information and final request to contact you

Example Six Third request

> Dear Ms. Ciara Harris,
>
> We have written to you twice on 10 May and 17 May respectively concerning your invoice No.S973203 in the amount of $2500.00, but have received neither your remittance nor

> *your explanation. The account is now 60 days past due. Enclosed you will find copies of the invoice and our two reminders. I am afraid your failure to settle the account will leave us no alternative but resort to legal proceedings.*
>
> *Please let us have your remittance for $2500.00 by May 30, after which our solicitors will take over the matter.*
>
> *Sincerely yours,*
>
> *Bright Chan*

Expressions to Learn and Remember

Terms to remember

account	due, overdue, past due, outstanding
payment	overdue payment, partial payment, full payment, payment schedule, be late with payments, ask for payment, send a payment request, payment reminder email, reduced payments in the amount of
invoice	late invoice, overdue invoice, charge 1.5% interest per month on late invoices
balance	outstanding balance, clear the balance
fee	late fee, charge a fee, waive a fee, add $166 in late fees to the invoice, charge fees on the outstanding balance

Sentence Patterns for Application

Requesting for payment

1. Please find the attached invoice for our services to you. The total amount is $1,200, payable via check, bank draft, or SWFT by March 10.
2. Our records show that you have an outstanding balance dating back to May 7. Please contact us or send your payment of $5,370 by May 14.
3. I enclose your statement as at 2 March which is overdue and I hope you will settle it as soon as possible.

4. This is the second letter I have sent you with regard to your outstanding account. As we haven't either a reply or remittance from you, we insist that you clear this account within seven days or at least offer an explanation for not paying it.

5. To avoid further late payments, you can contact your bank to set up a monthly transfer automatically on the 12th, which will reach us the same day, instead of physically mailing checks, which takes 7 days to arrive by post.

6. We shall expect to receive your full payment before May 1, or your explanation why the account is still outstanding.

7. However, if this payment has been made already, please disregard the email.

Explaining reasons for late payment & suggesting solutions

1. Because of the fire, we are in current difficulties in paying our supplier. Once our insurance company compensates us, we will send you our full payment.

2. Like many others, our business is severely impacted by the storm. We can only make partial payment on this account.

3. The workshop dispute held up our production and made it difficult for us to pay our suppliers promptly as usual.

4. According to my bank statement, $1538 has been debited from my current account.

5. When my financial situation improves, I will remit you the amount I owe you immediately. Thank you for your understanding.

6. When I received your letter of July 5 with my check attached marked "insufficient funds", I called my bank immediately and was told that the bank had failed to credit my account with a substantial deposit I had made several days prior. The bank will be sending you a formal letter of apology for their error.

Informing of late fees

1. We expect full payment for the amount of $1600 by the 1st of October 2012. Please note that a late fee of $15 will have to be added to it and appear on your next statement.

2. We will extend the credit for another week, after which a late fee will be charged.

3. We begin charging late fees on invoices after 15 days. Please clear the account in time to avoid paying extra.

4. Thank you for your business. Payment is due within 30 days. Please be aware that we will charge 1.5% interest per month on late invoices.

5. In accordance with the Late Payment of Commercial Debts Regulations 2018, we will add interest and late payment compensation to the sum outstanding. This is calculated based on the Bank of England base rate plus 8%.
6. If we need to work out smaller payments at regular intervals, we can discuss a plan and potentially waive any late fees.

Informing of possible consequences

1. If the invoice is not paid by the mentioned due date, we may suspend our services to you until such amount is paid in full.
2. I am afraid your failure to settle the account will leave us no alternative but to resort to legal proceedings.
3. Please let us have your check for $6500.00 by June 30, or our solicitor will take over the matter.
4. Because the overdue payment was not settled within the time frame, we have today turned the invoice together with all the other related documents over to a collection agency who will be in contact with you soon.
5. Please send us your remittance for $6,500.00 by June 30, after which we will begin legal action to recover the past due amount total, courts costs and statutory interest of 8% above the People's Bank of China base rate.
6. I will allow 10 business days for you to make payment arrangements, until 30 May. If I do not hear back, I will be submitting this against you in small claims court.
7. In view of our long-standing relations we are giving you a further seven days to clear the outstanding account, after which the matter will be dealt with by our solicitors.

Samples for Comprehension

❖ Sample One Payment Request 1

Dear Mr. Carter,

Subject: Payment Request for October Statement

We are writing with reference to the outstanding April statement for $7,030, which should have been cleared three weeks ago. Enclosed is a copy of the statement.

Our chief accountant Mr. Lyons is a little concerned that the bill has not yet been paid, and he wonders if you would like to discuss it with him.

Please call Mr. Lyons at your earliest convenience.

Yours sincerely,

Ms Sandy Lingerly
Secretarial Assistant

Enclosure: Statement

❖ Sample Two Payment Request 2

Dear Jack Lee,

In spite of the email payment reminder sent to you on August 10, we have not yet gotten a reply nor received your remittance. The account is now 14 days past due and you owe a total of $3,780.00.

When we allowed you credit facilities, we made it clear that payment should be settled promptly, and late payments could damage your credit ratings.

We shall expect to receive full payment before Sept 1, or your explanation why the account is still outstanding.

You may also want to contact us to work out a mutually agreeable payment schedule.

We look forward to hearing from you as soon as possible.

Yours sincerely,

Andrea Kingsbury

Chief Accountant

❖ Sample Three Reply to Payment Request

Dear Richard,

I was surprised to receive your letter of 20 November in which you said you had not received payment for invoice No. 74534.

On 2nd November I instructed my bank, the Chase Bank, Huntsville, to credit your account in Bank of China, Guangzhou, with $3,160. As my bank statement showed the amount had been debited to my account, I assumed that it had been credited to your account as well.

Could you please check this with your bank, and if there are any problems let me know, so that I can make enquiries here?

Thank you for your patience and cooperation.

Sincerely yours,

Bernin Smith
Sales Manager

❖ Sample Four Apology for Oversight

Dear Mr. Lowe,

Thank you for your email and the screenshot of the bank transfer, which showed that your account had been paid in full.

While we are very sorry for the inconvenience this has caused you, the enclosure of the screenshot enabled us to go through our records and pinpoint how this error on our part occurred.

Please accept our apology for the emails we wrote under the assumption that this bill had not been paid. I know this insistence on our part must have been extremely frustrating for you, especially in light of the fact that you have always been a valued customer of ours and have paid your bills promptly.

Thank you for your patience and please be assured that we will do everything in our power to ensure that this type of error does not occur in the future.

Yours sincerely,

Tony Brook

❖ Sample Five Following up Two Payment Reminders

Dear Mrs. Loong,

We wrote to you twice concerning your credit account with us, and we have received neither your payment nor your explanations so far.

A previous reminder was sent to you on 7 February, 2020, stating that the account was one week past due. Then two weeks later on February 21, 2020, we wrote to you again, notifying you that a weekly interest of 3% would be added to the account until payment was made.

With your current outstanding balance of $7,500 and interest charges of $150, your total amount due is $7,650.

Please clear the account within the next 10 days to avoid possible legal proceedings.

Sincerely yours,

John Merto

Financial Manager

❖ Sample Six Threatening Legal Actions

Dear Mr. Copper,

In spite of our repeated payment reminders on 3 and 17 June, and our request for payment by the deadline of 24, your account remains outstanding. Attached you will see the invoice detailing the outstanding sum you owe.

On 26 May we completed the remodeling of your store, according to our agreement.

The total balance that is currently due is $6,570.00. It is important that I hear what your plans are for paying this balance.

We will allow you another 7 business days to settle the account. If I do not get the payment within the time frame, I will be submitting this against you in small claims court.

I look forward to hearing from you soon.

Sincerely,

Jane Rochester

Tasks to Fulfill

1. Can you answer the questions?

(1) What should you do to avoid bad debt?
(2) What is the overall tone you should adopt in your first request for late payments?
(3) When should you take legal actions to recover the debt?
(4) What are the advantages of arbitration over legal action?

2. Read and answer the following questions.

Dear Ms. Fiona Frame,

I am contacting you again with reference to your outstanding payment on invoice No.74528 for our IT support services from January to July 2020. The invoice is now two weeks past due, and the amount you owe is $4,000. I would like to remind you that there is a late fee of $500 for all invoices after 30 days.

If you have any questions, please inform me; if not, please kindly send us the remittance as soon as possible. I am enclosing another copy of the invoice to this email in case you missed the original one.

Your prompt response will be appreciated. Thank you.

Kind regards,

John Smith

Encl.

Questions:

(1) Did Mr. Smith inform Ms. Fiona Frame of the past due account prior to this reminder?
(2) How much does Ms. Fiona Frame owe Mr. Smith?
(3) How much will Ms. Fiona Frame have to pay 30 days after the invoice date?
(4) Is anything enclosed in the letter?
(5) Which words in the letter have a similar meaning to the following?
   A. with reference to   B. unpaid   C. payment   D. send

3. Fill in the blanks to complete the letter.

We have written to you twice concerning your outstanding account which (1)_____ (过期) for more than four weeks, but we have received neither your reply nor your remittance. I am afraid your failure (2)_____ (付清欠款) will leave us no alternative but (3)_____ (诉诸法律措施).

This is to notify you that (4)_____ (除非我们收到您的支票) for $7,570.50 by June 30, the matter (5)_____ (此事将交由) our solicitors.

Self-evaluation

1. Can you translate the following expressions into English?

(1) 请求付款　　　(2) 延长付款时间　　(3) 过期未付的发票　　(4) 按期结算
(5) 汇款　　　　　(6) 支付计划　　　　(7) 托收机构　　　　　(8) 采取法律措施
(9) 小额索赔法庭　(10) 迟付货款滞纳金　(11) 额外的费用　　　　(12) 未结的账款
(13) 尽快付全款　　(14) 银行转账　　　　(15) 今天到期　　　　　(16) 限期结清
(17) 部分还款　　　(18) 催促付款　　　　(19) 原发票　　　　　　(20) 追讨欠款

2. Please translate the sentences into English.

(1) 友情提示，您的账户已经过期 7 天。

(2) 我们的记录显示您有一笔 5 月 12 日的未清余额。

(3) 您的欠款为 643 美元，现已到期，我们还没有收到这笔款项。

(4) 请联系我们，或于 2020 年 4 月 16 日之前支付我们 6100 美元。

(5) 请注意，发票逾期 30 天后将收取滞纳金。

(6) 请您尽快给我们一张银行汇票以结清这笔款项。

(7) 110702 号发票现已逾期 30 天。根据我们的协议，从明天开始每天滞纳金为 30 美元。

(8) 在此给您写信告知您，您 10 月未付的账单为 620 美元(附上影印件)，这笔款项应该在两周前结清。

(9) 我们想您也许没有看到金额为 935 美元的 50229 号发票（见副本），该发票日期为 11 月 11 日，12 月 10 日已到期。

(10) 你方尚欠我们 3780 美元，该款已逾期三个月以上，为此我们曾两次致函给你方，但我们既未收到回信，也未收到汇款。

(11) 附件是我们为您提供服务的发票，总金额为 1200 美元。请于 3 月 10 日前用支票、银行汇票或微信支付。

（12）我们一个主要的客户因为破产而无力支付我们的货款，我们也因而很遗憾无法在合约规定的日期内结清账款。

（13）请再延长我们的还款日期两个星期，我愿意为此支付 2% 的额外利息。

（14）很遗憾地通知您，在 4 月 30 日之前，或者我们收到全部账款，或者我们双方制订出一个双方都能接受的付款计划，否则我们将诉诸法律。

（15）一旦我们财务状况转好，我立刻付清欠款。

3. Please translate the sentences into Chinese.

(1) We are sure you enjoyed the shipment of books sent last week. However, we have not received the amount of $300 within the time stipulated in the contract.

(2) Enclosed you will find the outstanding May account/statement which should have been cleared a month ago.

(3) This is a reminder to pay your dues. If payment has been made please disregard this notice.

(4) We think you may have overlooked invoice No.5 for $895 which was due last month. Could you please send us your remittance to clear the amount as soon as possible?

(5) We would appreciate it if you could clear the account as soon as possible, as we ourselves have suppliers to pay.

(6) I have enclosed a self-addressed envelope for your convenience should you choose to send a check in the mail.

(7) Since we have received neither your response nor your remittance, we have forwarded your account to a collection agency.

(8) You have an outstanding payment of $1,600 on the invoice No. A852 which was due on the 14th of August, 2019. Please find enclosed a copy of the invoice for your reference.

(9) If the invoice is not paid by the mentioned due date, we may suspend our services to you until such amount is paid in full.

(10) Would you please instruct your bank to debit your account with HK$50,000 and transfer it to my account with The Hong Kong and Shanghai Banking Corporation Limited, Shanghai before the end of February?

(11) As agreed upon in our conversation, I will make reduced payments in the amount of $600 on or before the 10th of each month for a period of 5 months.

(12) To avoid further late payments, you can contact your bank to set up a monthly transfer automatically on the 12th, which will reach us the same day, instead of physically mailing checks, which takes 7 days to arrive by post.

(13) When we allowed you credit facilities, we made it clear that payment should be settled

promptly, and late payments could damage your credit ratings.
(14) Unless you settle your account before the end of this month, my solicitors will be instructed to start proceedings to recover the debt.
(15) We regret this action, but we have not received a response from you in a timely manner despite several attempts to contact you.

Did you remain courteous in the mail?
Did you make any grammar mistake?
Did you make any spelling mistake?
Did you apply the correct business words and adopt proper patterns in your sentences?

4. Please write an email informing your customer of his overdue account.

> (1) a consignment of garden chairs ordered four weeks ago   (2) delivered on time
> (3) overdue   (4) copy of invoice   (5) settle within seven days

Did you inform the receiver of the outstanding balance?
Did you include the invoice number and date?
Did you mention the number of days past due?
Did you tell the customer explicitly what you expect from him?

You can move on to Unit Nine if you can complete the exercises satisfactorily.

Unit Nine

Transportation

Transport is an important part in international business. Goods are carried by means of road, rail, air or sea. Sea transport is the major mode of transportation due to its low freight. So, we lay an emphasis on sea transport in this chapter.

Shipment, one of the indispensable terms of sales contract, signifies the seller's fulfillment of the obligation to make delivery of the goods. Terms of shipment generally contain time of shipment, ports of shipment and destination, freight rate, shipping documents, partial shipment or transshipment, etc.

The shipment should come into effect neither too long nor too short a time after the contract is concluded. The time limit governing a shipment falls into three categories: The time of shipment can be set on a fixed date, e.g. before the end of July, on July 25; the time of shipment can be set in the near future, e.g. immediate shipment, prompt shipment; the time of shipment can be an indefinite date, e.g. shipment within 30 days after the date of receipt of the letter of credit, shipment subject to shipping space available.

The freight rates include the cost of carrying the goods from one port to another and that of loading the goods on to the ship in the port of shipment and unloading them at the destination port. They also include any harbor charges that the ship may incur. Factors that influence the rate charged for any particular type of cargo are the weight of the goods being shipped, the dimensions of the goods being shipped, the shape of the goods, ease of damage, ease of pilferage, need for refrigeration or other special conditions, direction of traffic.

Shipping documents are a set of official papers that are necessary when sending goods from one country to another. They include commercial invoice, packing list, weight memo, certificate of origin, certificate of inspection, bill of lading, insurance policy. With these shipping documents ready, the exporter will try to get payment for the goods shipped.

Partial shipment and transshipment are usually chosen by the exporter to deliver a given lot of contracted goods. Partial shipment refers that the goods are delivered more than once. Transshipment refers that the direct sailing from the port of loading to the port of destination is unavailable.

Letters of shipment are usually written for the following purposes: to request for freight rates and sailings, to reply to shipping enquiry, to urge an early shipment, to give shipping instruction, to give shipping advice, etc.

Unit Objectives

After learning the unit, students should be able to:
1. Understand basic elements involved in negotiating transportation clause;
2. Recognize and remember related expressions and sentence patterns;
3. Apply the above in their trade practices related to transportation.

Structure & Content

Letters regarding shipment are usually written for the following purposes:

❖ To Request for Freight Rates and Sailings

In an inquiry letter for fright rate and sailings, the writer describes the packing (note that size rather than weight will be the main concern of the carrier in this case), states the value of the consignment, and mentions a delivery time.
- *We intend to ship a consignment of 10 machine tools to New York next month. The consignment has been packed into 2 containers, and the invoiced value is $20,000.*
- *Each box weighs 10 kilos gross, and measures 30 × 20 × 15 cm. And it is essential that the consignment be delivered by the end of this month. Please let us have the particulars of your service and its freight charges.*
- *If you quote a competitive rate, we can promise you regular shipments.*
- *Our customer is in urgent need of this goods. Therefore, shipment before the end of June, 2020 is a firm condition.*
- *Please kindly provide your best rate from Shanghai to London.*

❖ To Reply to Shipping Enquiry

In a reply to shipping enquiry, the writer first expresses his thankfulness for receipt of the enquiry, then quotes for "picking up" and "delivering" the consignment, and lastly show desire for cooperation with the potential customer.
- *Thank you for your recent inquiry of 15 May. We are enclosing the latest freight rates for your review and are confident that this literature will provide many of the answers you have requested.*
- *From the literature you can see that we arrange shipments to any part of the world and we offer very competitive shipping rates.*
- *If there is additional information you would like to have regarding our services, please do not hesitate to contact us. We will be most happy to be of assistance.*

❖ To Urge an Early Shipment

In this kind of letter, the buyer should firstly draw the attention of the seller that the ordered goods have not been received yet or no news has been heard about shipment, and secondly reiterate the importance of punctual delivery and the possible loss a delayed delivery of the goods may entail, and lastly urge the shipment of the goods in a tactful way.

- *Referring to our previous letters and cables, we wish to call your attention to the fact that up to the present moment no news has come from you about the shipment under the captioned contract.*
- *As you have been informed in one of our previous letters, the users are in urgent need of goods contracted and are in fact pressing us for assurance of early delivery.*
- *Under the circumstances, it is obviously impossible for us to again extend L/C No. 2450, which expires on 10th August, and we feel it our duty to remind you of this matter again.*
- *As your prompt attention to shipment is most desirable to all parties concerned, we hope you will let us have your telegraphic shipping advice without further delay.*
- *When we placed the order with you, we emphasized that delivery by the end of June was a firm condition of this transaction and punctual shipment was of utmost importance because this order was from a very important client, with whom we are trying to establish a firm trading relationship.*

❖ To Give Shipping Instruction

Shipping instructions are sent by the buyer to the seller and usually include the following three parts. Firstly, the buyer tells the seller that the relevant L/C has been established. Secondly, the buyer then puts forward some instructions concerning the date of shipment, name of the vessel, or the quality of the products, and so on. In the last part, the buyer expresses good wishes or shows that he is expecting the shipping advice.

- *We are in receipt of your letter of 5th June, from which we understand that you have booked our order for 2,000 sets of IBM-99 computers and respective 300 pieces of color monitors, main boards and drivers.*
- *Since the purchase is made on CIF basis, you are to send the goods to Guangzhou by the end of August.*
- *As these goods are susceptible to shock, they must be packed in seaworthy cases capable of withstanding rough handling. The bright metal parts should be protected from water and dampness in transit by a coating of slushing compound that will keep out dampness, but will not liquefy and run off under changing weather conditions.*
- *We trust that the above instructions are clear to you and that the shipment will give the users entire satisfaction.*

❖ To Give Shipping Advice

In international trade the buyer sometimes sends the shipping instructions (including shipping requirements) to the seller. Sometimes the buyer will write to the seller for informing the seller of effecting shipment in time in case of shipment delay. After the shipment of the goods, the seller will send the buyer the Shipping Advice to inform the buyer the related shipment details, the contents of which are as follows: the date of shipment, the shipped goods, the way of shipment.

- *We have shipped your order today.*
- *Please inform us with certainty when you can ship the goods so that we can promise a definite time of delivery to our*

customers.
- The goods we ordered are urgently required/in need and we request you to ship them by the first available vessel.
- You are requested to inform us immediately when shipment can be effected so that our customers may plan their production schedule.
- We will be able to make shipment of your order within 29 days after receipt of your L/C.
- Please let us have your shipping instructions immediately so that we can arrange to make shipment.
- The shipping date is coming near and please open your L/C urgently.
- In order to book shipping space, we have to take a shipping order from the shipping company.
- On finishing shipment, we will fax you the shipping advice.
- A full set of shipping documents are required for negotiation.

Expressions to Learn and Remember

Terms to remember

Means of transportation	road transport, rail transport, air transport, sea transport
Vehicles	ship, vessel, truck, lorry, van, train, liner, airliner, tramp
Ships/Vessels	steam ship (S.S.), motor vessel (M.V.), passenger ships, cargo ships, general cargo ships, bulk cargo ship, container ships, roll on/roll off ships, ferry boat, oil tanker, liquefied natural gas carrier, barge/lighter, pleasure boat/ship, tug boat, motor boat
Parties to a shipping contract	consignor/shipper, consignee, assign, assignor, assignee carrier, shipping company, shipping broker, forwarding agent, freight forwarder, freight company
Shipping documents	B/L, consignment note, air waybill, shipping advice/note, shipping order, freight invoice, certificate of origin, import license
Effecting shipment	send, dispatch, consign, deliver, carry, transport, ship, make delivery, take delivery

Sentence Patterns for Application

Arrangement for shipping

1. We intend to ship a consignment of 30 tea sets of crockery to London at the beginning of next month. The consignment has been packed in five crates, five sets per crate.
2. In reply to your letter of 8 July, I'll arrange for picking up and delivering your consignment from your address to the consignee's premises. Before signing the delivery note, could you please check that the consignment is complete and undamaged?
3. The first available vessel we can use to ship your No.5 consignment is the SS Northeast, which sails on 3 May and is due in London about 10 June. The vessel will stay here for 7 days and accept cargo from 17 April.
4. Could you please make the necessary arrangements for 20 electric typewriters to be shipped to Shanghai and handle all the shipping and insurance formalities/shipping formalities and insurance?
5. We have packed (and) ready the consignment. You are asked to ship and please let us know by return of post the earliest vessel leaving/sailing for Australia.
6. Please keep informed by this email that we have made all the necessary arrangements for your consignment to be loaded onto the SS Red Cross which sails for New Zealand on 4 June. I have also enclosed a check in payment of your freight account.
7. This consignment is destined for London and should be packed in a half-height container which measures in meters 6.1 x 2.4 x 1.2. We would advise you to take out the/an all risk insurance policy.
8. The shipping marks on the sides of the packing should entirely correspond with those on the shipping documents.
9. Please note that the ship closes for cargo on 5 April, and the freight is calculated by cubic meter. As for the sailing date, I think it suits your schedule for delivery.

Chartering a ship

1. We are pleased to inform you that we have been able to secure a bulk ship for you to charter, which has a cargo capacity of ten thousand tons and a speed of 20 knots and which will certainly be able to make fast turn round along the eastern coast.
2. At present we have an option on a vessel, the SS Orient, which can be hired/chartered for one voyage, sailing from Shanghai to Dalian. Considering that she is larger than you wanted, her owners are willing to offer a part charter of her, thus enabling you to share the cost.

Samples for Appreciation

❖ Sample One Enquire for Shipping

Dear Sirs,

We intend to ship a consignment of six writing desk assembly kits packed in six wooden cases measuring 60x40x20cm New York.

Could you inform us which vessels are available to reach New York before the end of next month and let us know your freight rates for picking up and delivering our consignment from the address of No.2 Linggong Road, Ganjingzi District, Dalian to the port New York?

Yours faithfully,

Paul Gary

Questions:

1. What are the details of the packing of the shipment?
2. What information does Paul Gary want to know about cargo transportation?

❖ Sample Two Quote for Shipping

Dear Mr. Lee,

Thank you for your enquiry of 21 May. Attached you will find details of our sailings for the beginning of next from Shanghai to New York.

You will see that the first available vessel will be the Dongfeng Orient which will accept cargo from 3 June to 7 June. The ship will arrive at New York on 3 June.

Our freight rate for crated consignments is £20.00 per ton, and attached please find our shipping instructions.

Yours sincerely,

Jerry Smith

Questions:

1. When will Mr. Lee's cargo leave Shanghai?
2. How much does the shipping company charge?
3. What is attached with the letter?
4. Which word in the letter correspond to shipping charges?

❖ Sample Three Urge Shipment

> Dear Mr. Lee,
>
> We are writing to remind you that the time for shipment of our order No.549 has long been overdue.
>
> Your delay has caused us much inconvenience and we must now ask you to dispatch the first 500 sets under this order by air to ensure prompt delivery, and the remaining 2,500 sets of the consignment by sea without further delay.
>
> Yours truly,
>
> Gary Zonk

Questions:

1. What is the status of order 549?
2. What is the exact time when we confirm the transaction?
3. What changes have been made to the mode of transport caused by the delay?

❖ Sample Four Contact a Forwarding Agent Shipment

> Dear Mr. Simpson,
>
> Could you please pick up a consignment of 20 computers and make the necessary arrangements for them to be shipped to Mr. M Tanner N. Z. Business Machines Company, 57 South Street, Wellington, New Zealand?
>
> Would you please handle all the shipping formalities and insurance and send us seven copies of the bill of lading, five copies of the commercial invoice, and the insurance certificate? We will advise our customers of shipment ourselves and would appreciate it if you could treat the matter as urgent. Your charges may be sent to us in the usual way.
>
> Yours sincerely,
>
> N Smith
> Senior Shipping Clerk

Questions:

1. What types of documents are involved in this shipment?
2. Who will pay the charges?
3. What does the consignment consist of?
4. Which words in the letter correspond to the following: collect; deal with; transported?

❖ Sample Five Advice Partial Shipment

Dear Ms. Clinton,

Your Order No. 310689 of dinner sets

Please be informed that 6 crates containing 24 dinner sets have been picked up from our warehouse by UPS this morning and will reach you within the next 7 days.

The remaining 24 sets will be loaded on ss Sea Pearl. She is due to leave Dalian for Boston on 20 November. We will keep you informed of her latest movements.

Thank you for your order and we hope you will be pleased with the dinner sets.

Yours sincerely,

Jiayin Li

Questions:

1. How many dinner sets will be delivered to Ms. Clinton by UPS?
2. When will the remaining goods leave Dalian?

Tasks to Fulfill

scan for the keys

1. Can you answer the questions?

(1) What are the four types of ocean shipping available in international trade?
(2) What kinds of cargo ships are available in ocean shipping?
(3) What are the factors that influence the rate charged for any particular type of cargo?
(4) What would be the main purposes of writing letters regarding shipment?

2. Read and answer the following questions.

Dear Ms. Jensen,

L/C No.7364 — Your Order No.5718 300 sets of Safety Pin Machine

We are pleased to advise you that 500 sets of Safety Pin Machine were put on flight CA 936 leaving Hong Kong 08:00, 9 May arriving Heathrow 14:00.

Please find attached air waybill DC946529 and copies of invoice A113/3.

Regarding the remaining 250 sets, we will try to hurry shipment and will advise you as soon as it is effected.
We appreciate the business you have been able to secure for us and assure you that all your further enquiries and orders will continue to receive our most careful attention.

Yours sincerely,

F. Crane

Questions:

(1) Is the writer an exporter or importer?
(2) What's the purpose of the writer in writing this letter?
(3) What documents are attached with the letter?
(4) How does the writer express his desire for further cooperation?

3. Fill in the blanks to complete the letter.

  Thank you for your fax of July 22 in which you asked whether we could (1)_____ (运送至香港) 20 crates of cigarette by 15th of August, 2022.
  I am sorry to tell you that shipment could only be (2)_____ (运送) in September. Nevertheless, if you desire (3)_____ (早点运达), we can make (4)_____ (分批运输) of ten crates in August and the remaining ten in September.
  Please let us know your decision as soon as possible, as it is difficult to (5)_____ (预定舱位) on account of the pandemic.

Self-evaluation

1. Can you translate the following expression into English?

(1) 装船通知　　(2) 航运船舶　　(3) 内燃机船　　(4) 客货船
(5) 杂货船　　(6) 集装箱船　　(7) 登记吨位　　(8) 发货人/托运人
(9) 装货港　　(10) 接货地　　(11) 运费　　(12) 租船契约
(13) 装船通知　　(14) 迟交　　(15) 散装　　(16) 转运，中转
(17) 分批装运　　(18) 不许转运　　(19) 海运提单　　(20) 目的港

2. Please translate the sentences into English.

(1) 有100台计算机，打包成10个木箱，尺码为60cm×40cm×20cm，货存在我公司开发区5号仓库，需发运到天津，请报价。

(2) 从香港驶往阿姆斯特丹的最早的轮船是"东方号"，将于6月5日驶离香港并大约于7月10日抵达阿姆斯特丹港。该轮将在这里停靠7天。从5月28日起装载你的货物。我们将负责办理所有装运和保险手续。

(3) 我们很高兴地通知您，我们已经找到了一艘散装货船供您租用。该轮载重量为5万吨，航速20节，符合您从澳大利亚往中国运送铁矿砂的要求。

(4) 所定货物因迫切需要，故请贵方加速装运。

(5) 请确保我们的货物由10月15日左右起航的"天山"轮装运。

(6) 贵公司应在货物备妥后15到20天之内派船到装货口岸。

(7) 从交货到零售商收到货物总共需要4到5个星期。

(8) 您是不是想把货物由香港转至澳门？

(9) 我们在香港转船去东南亚国家的货物途中未曾遇到过麻烦事。

(10) 有时因为在生产国找不到合适的装港，我们不得不转船。

(11) 据我所知，在香港转船期间有货物被盗或损坏的风险。

(12) 所有的转运费用都包括在到岸价格里面了。

(13) 我听说不允许分批装运。

(14) 货物必须 9 月份到达此地以便再转运。

(15) 我方已将货物装上 12 月 14 日开往贵方港口的"红星轮"。

Did you make any grammar mistakes?

Did you make any spelling mistakes?

Did you apply the correct business words and adopt proper patterns in your sentences?

3. Please translate the sentences into Chinese.

(1) The order No. 105 is so urgently required that we have to ask you to speed up shipment.

(2) Please make serious efforts to get the goods dispatched with the least possible delay.

(3) The users are in urgent need of the goods contracted and are in fact pressing us for assurance of an early delivery.

(4) We shall appreciate it if you will effect shipment as soon as possible, thus enabling our buyers to catch the brisk demand at the beginning of the season.

(5) Is it possible to effect shipment during March?

(6) The cargo has been shipped on board Dong Feng.

(7) Please advise us 30 days before the month of shipment of the contract number, name of commodity, quantity, port of loading and the time when the goods reach the port of loading.

(8) We regret we can't ship as you desired.

(9) Much to our regret, we cannot ship the goods within the time limit of the L/C owing to the unforeseen difficulties on the part of mill.

(10) The duplicate shipping documents including bill of lading, invoice, packing list and inspection certificate were airmailed to you today.

(11) We ship most of our oil in bulk.

(12) If there is any chance of the goods arriving late at this port by the specified date, we shall ask you to cancel the order. Your confirmation on this point would be appreciated.

(13) We hereby inform you that you should be held responsible for any losses arising from late delivery and improper packing.

(14) As the goods have not yet been dispatched, we must ask you to ship them without any further delay. If the order is not executed within the stipulated time, we shall have to cancel it.

(15) We have been doing everything possible to execute your shipment within the next week. In the meantime, we offer our apologies for the inconvenience this unfortunate delay has cause you.

4. Can you write a letter requesting freight rates and sailings according to the details given below?

(1) manufacturer of electric appliances
(2) ship 60 washing machines and 40 driers to Miami
(3) freight rates and sailings to London by 16, April, 2022
(4) have been packed into wooden crates
(5) marked with company logo and addresses
(6) The cargo should reach Miami before the end of next month

Did you introduce the goods you want to ship?
Did you mention your destination port and reaching time?
Did you enquire about the freight rate?

You can move on to Unit Ten if you can complete the exercises satisfactorily.

Unit Ten

Insurance

Insurance is an essential procedure in international trade. The insured can obtain the guarantee from the insurance company (the insurer) to get compensation of the cargo damaged or lost in transit at a relatively small cost, namely the insurance premium.

In international trade, sea transportation accounts for the biggest share in international cargo transportation. Therefore, marine insurance has become the most important insurance. Arrangements for sea shipments insurance may be made by either the buyer or the seller, in accordance with the terms of sale. In FOB and CFR terms, the importer is responsible for the insurance of the goods. In CIF term, the exporter is responsible for the insurance. Marine insurance is normally paid at the rate of 110% of the commercial invoice value of the goods.

The Basics of Cargo Coverage include "All Risk" coverage, General Average, With Particular Average (WPA), Free of Particular Average (FPA), War Risk, Inherent Vice and Warehouse-To-Warehouse protection.

Parties involved in an insurance contract are mainly the insurer, the insurance company, the insured. An insurer is one who, or that which, insures; the person or company that contracts to indemnify losses for a premium and especially an insurance underwriter. An insurance company is a financial institution that sells insurance. It has the following synonyms: insurance firm, insurer, insurance underwriter, underwriter. The insured in the insurance contract refers to the person, group, or property for which an insurance policy is issued.

Unit Objectives

After learning the unit, students should be able to:
1. Understand basic elements involved in negotiating insurance clause;
2. Recognize and remember related expressions and sentence patterns;
3. Apply the above in their trade practices related to insurance.

Structure & Content

❖ Asking for Relevant Information About Terms of Insurance

We would like to know if you could offer a comprehensive insurance policy covering us against fire, flood, accident, industrial injury, and theft.

I'm writing to ask whether your insurance company allows the foodstuffs to be insured against the risk of deterioration.

We want to know your lowest rates FPA.

Please kindly quote us your rate for the insurance coverage.

❖ Acknowledge Receipt of the Letter on Insurance Matters

Thank you for your letter of 16 March. With regard to your inquiry on insurance, we are pleased to provide the following details.

Thank you very much for your letter of 6 April in which you enquired about our insurance cover.

❖ Offering Relevant Information About Insurance

Many export-oriented Chinese manufacturers choose to insure their consignment with the PICC.

Unless otherwise regulated in the L/C, the negotiation bank will permit the beneficiary/exporter to deliver either of Insurance Policy, Insurance Certificate and Open Policy for negotiation.

I have enclosed leaflets explaining our three fully-comprehensive industrial policies which offer the sort of cover you require, and I think that policy A351 would probably suit you best as it offers the widest protection at 65% with full indemnification.

❖ Express Your Willingness to Insure the Goods

If our rate is acceptable, please let us know immediately so that our insurance policy can reach you in time.

I look forward to receiving your confirmation that these terms are acceptable.

❖ Claim of Damage

We would like to inform you that a fire broke out in the basement of our warehouse yesterday. Although the blaze was brought under control, we estimate that about £4000.00 worth of stock was badly damaged.

A fire brigade officer informed us that the blaze was probably caused by an electrical short which he thought must have occurred around midnight. Fortunately, though, the brigade's action prevented extensive damage.

I would be grateful if you could send us the necessary claims forms.

❖ Reply to Claim for Damage

I now have the report from our surveyor, Mr. Nutty, who visited your premises on 18 October to inspect the damage caused by the fire on the 15th.

From the copy of the report enclosed you will see that although he agrees that the fire was probably caused by an electrical fault, he feels that £2.000.00 is a more likely evaluation for damage to stock at present market prices.

However, he suggests that we also pay a further £600.00 for structural damage to your premises. Consequently, we are prepared to offer you a total of £2.60.00 in full compensation under your policy.

If you accept this assessment, would you please fill out the enclosed claims form and return it to us with a letter confirming acceptance of the compensating we have offered?

Expressions to Learn and Remember

Terms to remember

Process	application, proposal form, applicant, the insured; the insurer, cover note, insurance certificate, insurance policy; premium, value insured, invoice value plus 10%, 110% of the invoice value, warehouse-to-warehouse protection; claim, make/file a claim on/for ... with, claimant, claim form, declaration form, surveyor, adjuster, survey report, inspect damage, make an assessment, compensation/indemnification; arbitration, arbitrator, umpire, final and binding arbitration award; subrogation
Parties involved	applicant, the insured, the insurer, insurance broker, insurance company, underwriter, claimant, adjuster, surveyor, assessor, independent assessor/ surveyor, arbitrator
Risks, danger and perils	damage (to), loss, total loss, partial loss, general average, particular average, natural calamities, fortuitous accident, catastrophe, disaster, force majeure, fire, collision, inherent vice

Cover(age)	life insurance/assurance; property insurance; fire insurance; accident insurance, personal accident insurance; insurance of liability; insurance of interest Marine insurance: FPA (Free from Particular Average), WPA (With Particular Average), All Risks, War Risks, Extraneous/Additional Risks, Civil Commotion Risks, Strike Risks Standard clauses, Institute clauses
Documents involved	proposal form, cover note, insurance certificate, insurance policy, survey report, arbitration award insurance policy: valued/unvalued policy; time policy, voyage policy, mixed policy; floating policy; open cover (policy)

Sentence Patterns for Application

Application for coverage of risks

1. As our present policy runs out at the end of this month and the insurance rates that our former insurers are charging are too high, we would like to know if you could offer a comprehensive insurance policy covering us against fire, flood, accident and theft. So a competitive quotation will be appreciated.
2. Our premises, along with the fixtures and fittings, are valued at £150,000. There have been no open fires and floodings on the premises since the factory went into operation / we began trading ten years ago. We have never had claims for industrial injury either.
3. In answer to your enquiry of 6 April, I'm pleased to inform you that the kind/sort of insurance cover you require is Policy A361, which offers a comprehensive/the widest protection against all risks at a rate of 65% (with full indemnification).
4. Our Personal Accident Scheme could best satisfy your requirements and covers your students during the entire period of the Inter-college Basketball Games in London for a maximum of up to £30,000.
5. As Mr. Cade has an excellent record, we agree to cover him under Fidelity Bonds for £20,000 on the understanding/condition that he will only handle credit cards and customers' accounts.
6. As the matter is urgent, we would appreciate your prompt reply to give us details with regard to packing and price lists.

7. Thank you for your letter of the 5th in which you asked about cover for a shipment of computers from Shanghai to Bangkok. Please find enclosed a cover note/proposal form/declaration form which should be completed and returned to us.

8. As we will be making regular shipments to the seaborne ports along the Southeastern Asian coast, we would like to know if you could arrange open cover for a total of £400,000 against All Risks. We look forward to learning from you.

9. An open cover for a total of £10,000 has been arranged at a rate of 3%. I am enclosing a block of declaration forms and you are required to submit one for each shipment made.

10. As our present policy runs/expires/is due at the end of this month and we are not going to renew it with our former insurer who charges too high insurance rates, we would like to know if you could offer a comprehensive property insurance policy covering our premises along with fixtures and fittings against fire, flood, accident and theft. Our premises are valued at $2 million. No dangerous situations whatsoever have happened since the factory went into operation.

Claims

1. We regret to inform you that a fire broke out at No.1 warehouse yesterday at midnight and the blaze was brought under control ten minutes later by the fire brigade. We estimate that about £3,000 worth of stock was damaged/the loss to the stock at £3,000.

2. The report from our surveyor shows that £2,000 is a more likely evaluation for damage/loss to your stock. Consequently, we are prepared to offer you a total of £2,000 in full compensation under your policy.

3. We shall pay the compensation for the two students injured during the intercollege football game. Please could you give us the details of how the accident occurred and how long they are expected to be kept from college in the hospital.

4. As for your claim of May 2, we'll consider the matter once we have full details of the survey report.

5. The B/L No.7 was claused with comments on ten broken packing cases, for which we have to file a claim with you.

6. The consignment delivered to our promises consisted of eight cases, two of which were found broken. We estimate the loss on invoice value to be £2,000 for which we claim compensation.

Samples for Comprehension

❖ Sample One Enquiry about Covering all Risks

> Dear Sir,
>
> We have 200 cartons of woolen sweaters to be shipped to Ms. Judith Jones, Bremer Enterprises, 47 Skyway Drive, New York. The consignment is to be loaded on to SS Hamburg, which leaves Tanggu on March 12 and is due in New York on March 30.
>
> The invoiced value of the consignment is $16,050.
> We would be grateful if you could quote a rate covering All Risks from port to port.
>
> Faithfully yours,
>
> *Francesca Pena*
> Export Manager

Questions:

1. When does the cargo ship leave and when will it arrive?
2. Does the exporter require the importer to provide port-to-port WPA?

❖ Sample Two Inquiry about Insurance Plan

> Dear Sirs,
>
> Our firm is currently looking for lower rates for a comprehensive insurance plan for our employees and for our business. We are a leading manufacturer of plastic products with a staff of 300 and our insurance needs are as follows:
>
> 1. Health Insurance.
>
> 2. Liability Insurance.
>
> 3. Policy to cover our equipment and machinery (a list of equipment and machinery and their value is attached) against fire, flood, accident and theft.
>
> Please review our current policy to see where we are currently covered, and which areas require coverage. Any suggestions for additional types of insurance would be welcomed. If you have any questions, please contact me.
>
> Yours truly,
>
> Issac Biden

Questions:

1. What is the purpose of the company's letter?
2. What projects does the company mainly operate?
3. Does the company want to participate in advertising insurance and sales insurance?
4. What is the policy on equipment and machinery mainly for?

❖ Sample Three Reply to Enquiry about Insurance Coverage

Dear Mr. Daracott,

Thank you for your letter of March 12 in which you enquired about our insurance coverage.

We offer a complete medical plan, including: Life and Accidental Death Coverage, $100.00 per individual, $300.00 per family deductible, 80% Major Medical with Stop Loss and $300.00 Accident Benefit.

I am sure that you will agree that the coverage we are offering is quite comprehensive and the rates quoted are very low.

For more information on Chambers Group Medical Plan, please call any of our service representatives at (739) 457-4488.

Yours sincerely,

Jim Smith

Questions:

1. What are the items included in the medical plan?
2. What are the advantages of the medical plan?
3. How to get more information on Chambers Group Medical Plan?

❖ Sample Four Claim of Damage

Re: Claim on crockery
Ref: Policy number CRT/345/678/HY

Dear Mr. Pearson,

As per our telephone conversation on October 12, I have put our losses in writing.

On October 1 our firm had five crates of crockery in our warehouse waiting to be picked up for delivery by COSCO Carrier. However, on October 6 a fire broke out and damaged the merchandise to be shipped.

Although the fire was brought under control very soon, we estimate that about RMB3000 worth of stock was damaged.

Please find attached invoice No. 62317, dated September 25, 2020, with a total amount of RMB6380. Our insurance should cover the damage to the items mentioned above.

Your immediate attention to this matter would be greatly appreciated.

Sincerely yours,

B. Renwick
Shipping Manager

Questions:

1. Were the five crates of crockery in the warehouse damaged by fire during transportation by COSCO?
2. How to carry on the claim for the inventory damage of RMB3000?
3. Is it a valid method fo the shipping manager to provide evidence by way of taking a video through We Chat?

❖ Sample Five Reply to Claim for Damage

Dear Mr. Renwick,

Thank you for your letter of April 23 which we received yesterday. Right now we are looking into the matter and we will let you have our decision as soon as we have full details.

Enclosed you will find the claim forms you requested in your letter.

Yours sincerely,

John Pearson

Questions:

1. How are we dealing with the matter at present?
2. What is enclosed in the letter?

Tasks to Fulfill

scan for the keys

1. Can you answer the questions?

(1) What does average mean in marine insurance?

(2) Does All Risks cover the insured against literally all risks?

(3) What's open cover policy?

(4) When is an open cover policy likely to be arranged?

2. Read and answer the following questions.

Dear Sirs,

　　As our present policy expires at the end of this month and the premiums that our former insurance company charged are too high, we would like to know if you could offer a comprehensive insurance policy covering us against fire, flood, accident and theft. Your competitive quotation will be appreciated.

　　When calculating the premium, would you please take the following into consideration:

　　We are a manufacturer producing safety goggles with a staff of thirty. Our premises, along with the fixtures and fittings, are valued at £150,000. There have been no open fires and flooding on the premises since the factory went into operation. We have never had claims for industrial injury either. Fire passages and fire extinguishers are placed as required.

Yours faithfully,

Mr. Cade

Questions:

(1) Why does Mr. Cade's company want to change its insurers?

(2) What sort of policy is Mr. Cade's company asking for?

(3) How many people does Mr. Cade's company employ?

(4) What precautions has Mr. Cade's company taken against fire?

(5) Which words in the letter have a similar meaning to the following?

　　A. runs out　　B. Insurance rate　　C. assessed

3. Fill in the blanks to complete the letter.

This is to (1)_____ (告知我方已经收到你方 3 月 20 日来函), asking us to insure the goods for an amount of 110 % above the invoice value.

We are pleased to inform you that we have covered the shipment with China Life Insurance (Group) Company against (2)_____ (一切险和战争险), for £10,000

The policy is being prepared (3)_____ (相应地) and will be forwarded to you by next Tuesday together with (4)_____ (保险费的索款通知).

The extra premium will (5)_____ (由你方负担).

Self-evaluation

1. Can you translate the following expressions into English?

（1）保险金额　　（2）仲裁裁定　　（3）平安险　　（4）预约保单　　（5）赔偿和赔款
（6）投保人　　　（7）保险证明　　（8）水渍险　　（9）浮动保单　　（10）保险代理
（11）保险金额　（12）分保　　　　（13）可保险权益（14）赔付　　　（15）险种
（16）海上保险　（17）全险　　　　（18）战争险　　（19）保险单　　（20）保费

2. Please translate the sentences into English.

（1）你们保险公司一般承包哪些险种？

（2）我们这批货如果以 CIF 价格成交，你们负责投保哪些险别？

（3）加保破碎险的费用由谁支付？

（4）请注意上述货物须在 6 月 15 日前装运，并按发票金额 150% 投保综合险。

（5）我们知道按一般惯例你们只按发票金额 110% 投保，因此额外保险费将由我们负担。

（6）兹收到你方 7 月 20 日来信，要求我们代办标题货物的保险，保险费由你方承担。

（7）我们高兴地通知你，我们已向中国人民保险公司为上述货物投保了一切险，投保金额为 £2,200。

（8）谢谢你方 6 月 16 日来信，要求我们承保从利物浦运至孟买的四箱精制皮制品。

（9）这笔保险的保险费是申报金额 £925 的 9‰。

（10）保险单正在准备中，2 到 3 天即可寄上。兹确认我们已从今天起承保这批货。

（11）我们想把下列商品按金额 £925 投保一切险，即四箱精制皮制品，唛头为 1-4。

（12）我们需要立即投保至孟买的保险，一俟保险单办妥，请即寄为荷。

（13）同时也请确认你方已承保上述货物。

(14) 保险单正在准备中，在本周末我们将把保险单连同收取保险费的通知一并寄给你们。

(15) 额外的保险费将由你方负担。

Did you make any grammar mistake?
Did you make any spelling mistake?
Did you apply the correct words and patterns in your sentences?

3. Please translate the sentences into Chinese.

(1) As requested, we can arrange insurance on your behalf.

(2) Insurance shall be covered by the seller for 110% of invoice value against All Risks.

(3) Please let us know the premium at which leakage is covered by the insurers on your side.

(4) Our usual practice is to insure shipments for the invoice value plus 10%.

(5) We have covered the goods against FPA and TPND.

(6) As agreed, we have covered the insurance on the 300 bolts of Printed Shirting for 110% of the invoice value against WPA with the People's Insurance Company of China.

(7) We can cover your goods against All Risks and War Risks. But at a slightly higher premium, the difference of which will be for your account.

(8) We are prepared to comply with your request and obtain cover for 150% of the invoice value. The extra premium will be for your account

(9) We shall, of course, refund the premium to you upon receipt of your debit note or, if you like, you may draw on us at sight for the amount required.

(10) For your reference, we have taken out an Open Policy with the People's Insurance Company of China.

(11) In the absence of your definite instructions regarding insurance, we covered your ordered goods against All Risks for 110% of the invoice value according to our usual practice.

(12) The premium for this cover is at the rate of 1% of the declared value of 5,500.

(13) The policy is being prepared and will be forwarded to you together with our debit note within this week.

(14) Please see to it that the above-mentioned goods should be shipped before October 25th and the goods should be covered for 125% of the invoice value against All Risks and War Risks.

(15) We know that according to your usual practice, you insure the goods only for 10% above the invoice value. Therefore, the extra premium will be for our account.

4. Can you write a reply to declaim for fire damage according to the details given below?

(1) An investigation has been made on 18, October by a surveyor, Mr. Kern.
(2) The fire was caused by an electrical fault.
(3) Assessment of the damage is about £2.000.00.

Did you give a brief report on the damage investigation you have made?
Did you make a damage assessment?
Did you put forward a compensation plan?
Did you ask for a letter confirming acceptance of the compensating you have offered?

You can move on to Unit Eleven if you can complete the exercises satisfactorily.

Unit Eleven
Complaints & Claims

A complaint letter informs the company that the customer is dissatisfied with the goods or services, and a claim is a complaint to inform the company of the problem and suggest a fair compensation. Most common causes for claims result from an incorrect bill, invoice, or statement, delivery of incorrect or damaged merchandise and unusually delayed delivery. No matter how infuriating the nature of the problem nor how great the inconvenience, the objective of the claim IS NOT to express anger, BUT to get results. Hostile or demanding tone is to be avoided.

Customer-to-business complaints and business-to-business complaints and claims are inevitable.

Complaints arise in spite of the careful performance of a contract by the exporter and importer. They are likely to be caused by various reasons such as more or less quantity delivered, wrong goods delivered, miscalculation, poor packing, inferior quality, discrepancy between the samples and the goods which actually arrived, delay in shipment, etc. Once disputes arise, arbitration is better than litigation, and conciliation is better than arbitration.

Unit Objectives

After learning the unit, when filing complaints, students should be able to:
1. Follow the right steps;
2. Adopt proper language of complaint;
3. Explain the mistake;
4. Suggest a solution to the problem.

Structure & Content

An effective complaint often contains the following steps: background, problem, solution, warning (optional) and closing.

After describing the background, the writer first points out the problem and then suggests a solution. The writers may even state his or her feelings, depending on how bad the problem is. Warning is occasionally needed. The writer often closes the letter with such expressions as "I look forward to hearing from you soon." Or "I will greatly appreciate your attention to this matter."

When pointing out the mistake and explaining the problem, the writer should remain polite and respectful. The tone of complaint letters should not be aggressive or insulting, as this would annoy the reader and not encourage him/her to solve the problem. Emotional terms like *disgusted, infuriated, or amazed* have no place in business.

❖ Introducing the Background

I am writing to complain about the wrong product I received today.

I am writing with reference to Order No. 275, which we received yesterday.

I am writing to inform you that the goods we ordered from your company have not been supplied correctly.

On March 17 we ordered a box of letterhead stationery for our central office in Springfield.

When we placed the order for 6 three-piece-suite with you on 10 April, you agreed to deliver it by 1 May.

On 25 November 30 boxes of electronic hand mixers were delivered to us with delivery note number 130.

I received a consignment of washing machines, Cat. No. DT154, to the above order yesterday.

I am writing to complain about the shipment of street light bulbs we received yesterday against the above order.

At the time of delivery, our shipping and receiving manager noticed 3 vases were broken. It was apparent to him that insufficient packing materials were the cause of the problem.

I am writing to complain about the wooden bridge which you built for my garden last August.

I am writing with reference to my June statement which you forwarded to me on July 10.

❖ Pointing out the Problem

We have now waited almost nine weeks and still have not received the books ordered with you.

Nine of the thirty boxes were broken from apparent mishandling.

However the delivery consisted of six MD100V332DG5 machines instead of the MG120VJ31DS3 machines I asked for.

We would like to inform you that the dressing tables we received today are not what we originally ordered.

There appears to be an error on the statement.

We have received your July statement for ￥3,280, but we have noticed it contains an error.

When the plastic bag was removed, I noticed some damage to my clothing. The shirt has a hole and the pants have changed color.

Only 600 of the total 1000 units ordered were delivered as per our contract. The partial shipment has caused delay in our building project.

The overall dressing gowns for which we have

been waiting in anticipation have not reached us as per our agreement, and we have not heard from concerning their shipment.

❖ Explaining the Problem

If you think you know how the mistake was made, you may politely point this out to your supplier.
Invoice Y1146 for ￥256.00 has been debited twice.

Upon checking the details of my June statement, I noticed that invoice No. 285 was debited twice and there is a charge for a consignment of frozen meat that we neither ordered nor received.

You have charged me for a delivery of woolen sweaters, invoice No. Y1162 for ￥3,550.00, but I neither ordered nor received them.

There seem to be some misunderstanding regarding terms of discount. Discount is deducted from net prices, not CIF prices.

I have been waiting in anticipation for my new hat now for several weeks. I have attached a copy of my receipt to show an ordering date of July 6. The hat is to be worn at my daughter's wedding at the end of September. As it is now August 18, I am afraid that the hat may have been misplaced.

The bookcases which were delivered in my absence were totally the wrong color.

The order may have been misplaced.

The mistake could not have originated here, and must be connected with the dispatch of the goods.

I think the reason that wrong sizes have been sent to me is that I am ordering in metric sizes, and you are sending me sizes measured in feet and inches. I would appreciate your looking into the matter.

The board we ordered from you (invoice No 64593) arrived two days after the promised delivery date, causing us to lose three more work days on our house construction.

❖ Suggesting a Solution

If you think you know how the mistake can be corrected, let your supplier know.

I would like to claim a free repair/replacement/refund.

Please pick up the wrong delivery and send us the items as per our purchase order No. 3852 by the end of the month.

I am therefore asking you to repair the item free of charge or to replace it with one that is working properly.

I send you a debit note for €984.00 and deduct it from my next statement, and that should put the matter right.

In addition, we expect reimbursement from you.

The quality of the suites is not acceptable. We have to return them, freight forward, and ask for either replacements or refund from you.

The best solution would be for me to return the wrong articles, charging you P&P.

Rather than send a credit note you could send six replacements, which would probably be easier than adjusting our accounts.

I am returning the stationery under separate cover, with the needed correction noted. I will appreciate your sending me the correct stationery as soon as possible. Also, I trust you will credit my account with $4.86, the cost of returning the stationery.

If you cannot deliver the wine by the end of the month, please cancel the order.

❖ Warning

This is usually not needed in the first contact. Otherwise, we may have to look elsewhere for our supplies.

We may be forced to place our orders with other suppliers.

Please put the matter right quickly to avoid possible damage and legal actions.

If the outstanding fees are not paid by 1 February 2021, you will incur a 10% late payment fee.

❖ Closing

Thank you for your attention to this matter.

I look forward to receiving your explanation of these matters.

I look forward to receiving your prompt reply.

I look forward to hearing from you soon.

Example

Dear Mr. Smith,	
The 100 cameras shipped via UPS were delivered to us yesterday.	Background
Upon examination 2 cameras in 2 cases were found severely damaged.	Problem
An independent surveyor's report suggests that the damage was caused by improper packing.	Cause of the problem
Since the transaction is on a CIF basis, we would like to get replacements or a refund in the sum of $3,200.	Claim
The damaged cameras are put aside for your inspection and instruction.	
I look forward to hearing from you soon.	Expectation
Sincerely yours,	
Tony Blair	

Expressions to Learn and Remember

Terms to remember

payment	overdue; penalty; receive payment
order	cancel the order, a wrong delivery to / against the order, order in metric sizes/in British ones
account	credit our account, terminate the account
shipment	postponed shipment; delayed shipment, expedite shipment, partial shipment, late shipment
quality	defective merchandise
delivery	late delivery, prompt delivery without further delay, expected date of delivery, postpone , complaint , wrongly delivered consignment / goods;
complaint	make a complaint about, make/file/lodge a claim with ... on/for, justified / unjustified complaint
damage	claim damages, found broken/ stolen to the value of; a list of damaged and missing goods
investigation	examine the case, to make an immediate inspection, to carry out a full investigation
compensation	compensate us for, demand a refund of $XXX for the time and money, request reimbursement, reimburse us for

Sentence Patterns for Application

Explaining the problem

1. I'm writing to complain about the shipment of sweaters we received yesterday against the above order. Thirty garments to the value of $6,000 have been stolen.
2. On 15 January 2021 we placed an order with you for 12,000 ultra super long-life batteries. The consignment arrived yesterday but contained only 1,200 batteries.
3. The chocolate you shipped to us last week arrived in bits and pieces.
4. You sent us an invoice for $10,532, but did not deduct the 5% quantity discount.
5. You said in your e-mail the LCD panels would be delivered this week. But we have not received them or heard from you since Sept. 2, 2020.

6. Attached you will find a list of the damaged and missing articles.
7. I think the reason the wrong sizes have been sent to me is that I'm ordering in metric sizes and you are sending me sizes measured in feet and yards.
8. On opening the hatch we found three boxes broken, in which most of the cases were smashed.
9. I have received your July statement for £ 3,280.54 but notice it contains a number of errors.

Suggesting a solution

1. Please kindly locate and return our missing items or compensate us for our losses the penalties that our general contractor has leveled against us due to your late delivery.
2. Please make up the shortfall as soon as possible and to ensure that such errors do not happen again.
3. Because your warehouse has not yet shipped my refrigerator, please cancel my order, credit and close my account, and take me off your mailing list.
4. We request that you reimburse us for the expenses.
5. We would appreciate your company sending us the remainder of the hardware we ordered.
6. We suggest you credit us for the issues I have not received.
7. The goods cannot be retailed even at a discount, so what we can only do is return them to you.
8. Could I please ask you to look into these matters?
9. Please send us a corrected invoice for $9,479, deducting our 15% discount.
10. I trust you will credit my account with $25.86, the cost of returning the goods.

Samples for Comprehension

❖ Sample One Complaint of Late Delivery

Dear Mr. Robinson,

The 10 woolen carpets we ordered with you on September 6 have not yet arrived. It is now more than 10 days overdue. According to the contract, late delivery will result in a penalty of $20 per day.

If you have shipped the goods, please provide us with the tracking number.

Should the consignment not reach us within the next week, we shall have no choice but to cancel the order. And we will have to ask for compensation for our losses.

Yours sincerely,

Michael Blackburn

Director

❖ Sample Two Complaint of Wrong Delivery

Dear Mr. Nicholas Butcher,

Re: Order No. 5940

On February 16, 2021, we placed an order with you for 6 projectors with sound system, and the order stated that delivery will be made within three weeks. Attached you will find a copy of the original order.

However, 10 printers instead of 6 projects were delivered to us this morning. As the projectors will be needed within four days, we request you send us the goods as per the order by air so that we can receive them within 48 hours. Otherwise we will have to cancel the order and make some emergency purchases to fulfill our commitments to our customer. And we shall hold you liable for all our losses, including but not limited to our reputation and sales.

Enclosed you will find a copy of our original order with you.

I am waiting for your prompt replacements.

Regards,

Elsa Chanson

❖ Sample Three Complaint of Poor Workmanship

Dear Mr. Carpenter:

The heavy wind yesterday ripped off several of the new shingles your workers installed for our new office. A close inspection of the damage reveals that the adhesive strip did not take hold as the plastic covering from the backs of the shingles had not been removed, and that only one nail had been used per shingle in many cases.

According to the standard building agreement, materials and workmanship are guaranteed for one year, so I expect the roof to be properly repaired as soon as possible since a year will soon be up and the rainy season is coming.

Please have the work completed by May 20 to avoid further damages.

Thank you for your attention to the matter.

Yours,

Mr. Pence

❖ Sample Four Complaint of Faulty Goods

Dear Mr. Lyons,

RE: Complaint about faulty cabinets delivered on April 2021

Upon the delivery of the 30 cabinets we ordered with you, we noticed some of the cabinet doors do not open and shut properly. Obviously they do not match the sample against which we placed the order with you. Please replace them with products of the same quality as the sample within the next 10 days and make arrangements to pick up the faulty ones at your cost.

Enclosed you will find some pictures of the problem cabinets.

Yours sincerely,

Jane Brown

Enclosed: pictures of the problem cabinets

❖ Sample Five Complaint of Improper Meals

Dear Mr. Mack Simons,

I am writing to complain about the one-day tour of the harbor city organized by your company.

After lunch my family and I did not feel well due to bad stomach pains. I was forced to take sick leave next day, and I am enclosing a copy of the doctor's note.

Due to the discomfort and inconvenience, I request compensation for the doctor's fees to the amount of $316.

I look forward to hearing from you.

Yours,

Bob Eiffel

Tasks to Fulfill

scan for the keys

1. Can you answer the questions?

(1) What is a customer complaint?

(2) What are the suggested steps in complaining?

(3) What is a claim?

(4) What manners should be adopted when complaining or claiming compensation?

2. Read and answer the following questions.

Re: Purchase Order No.14478

Dear Miss Higson,

I am writing to you to complain about the shipment of woolen hats we received yesterday against the above order.

The boxes in which the hats were packed were damaged, and looked as if they had been broken open in transit. From your invoice No.18871 we estimate that 12 hats have been stolen, to the value of $600.00. Because of the rummaging in the boxes, quite a few other hats were crushed or stained and cannot be sold as new articles in our shops.

As the sale was on a C&F basis and the forwarding company was your agents, we suggest you contact them with regard to compensation.

You will find a list of the damaged and missing articles enclosed, and the consignment will be put to one side until we receive your instructions.

Yours sincerely,

Peter Burke
Chief Buyer

Encl.

Questions:

(1) How did the damage occur?

(2) How many hats are stolen?

(3) How much are the stolen hats worth?
(4) What is enclosed with the letter?
(5) Why does Mr. Burke put the hats in his warehouse?
(6) Which words in the letter have a similar meaning to the following?
   A. during transportation   B. assess   C. get in touch with

3. Fill in the blanks to complete the letter.

Dear Mr. Button:

Re: (1)_____ （728 号订单）

(2)_____ (我们订购了贵厂 300 套早餐桌和椅子) on 18 May after we visited your factory in Horseshoe, Oxford. As agreed, delivery is expected to be made within 4 weeks receipt of the order. However, four weeks have passed and (3)_____ (我们还是没有收到这批货物).

Unless we receive the goods within the next five days, (4)_____ (我方将不得不取消订单). We would like to make it clear that we are holding you liable to your delivery contract, and (5)_____ (我方将要求你方赔付我们可能遭受的损失)

Bernin Smith
Sales Manager

Self-evaluation

1. Can you translate the following expressions into English?

(1) 投诉
(2) 按照合同规定
(3) 违约
(4) 与……不符
(5) 计算错误
(6) 错发的货物
(7) 部分货物
(8) 受损货物清单
(9) 被计价两次
(10) 做工粗劣
(11) 索赔
(12) 要求退款
(13) 替换质量有问题的货物
(14) 采取法律措施
(15) 解决纠纷
(16) 避免类似的错误
(17) 退还货物
(18) 原始收据
(19) 纠正错误
(20) 经调查发现

2. Please translate the sentences into English.

(1) 今天收到了我们 8 月份的账单，我方认为账单上的数额与应付数额不同。

(2) 您收取了我一批油漆的货款，可是我既没有订购油漆也没有收到油漆。

(3) 我写此函向贵公司投诉你方 5 月 4 日错发来给我的 3 号订货。

(4) 请立即核查此事并告知我方你们的处理意见。

(5) 天津轮运来的货物中 2 包丢失，价值大约 2 千美元的服装被偷盗。

(6) 我们收到的服装与订货时所凭的样品不符，且差异超出允许范围。我们要求退货。

(7) 随函附上丢失和受损货物的清单一份。

(8) 我们订购的货物又一次没有按期交货，这是今年的第二次了，我们很失望。

(9) 除非你方给出合理的解释并采取必要的补救措施，否则订货将取消。

(10) 我们将多发的货物退给您，邮费由你方承担。

(11) 最好的解决办法是我方将错发的货物返还给您，然后再发给您一张索款单来调整账目。

(12) 破损的瓷器已放置在一边供您来检查。

(13) 请通知你方银行将 50000 港元从你方账户中转入我方在中国银行大连分行的账户中，以弥补差价。

(14) 请尽快把我们订购的轮胎给我们送来，并取走错发的货物。

(15) 如果因此而造成重大损失，我方将采取法律行动。

Did you make any grammar mistake?
Did you make any spelling mistake?
Did you apply the correct business words and adopt proper patterns in your sentences?

3. Please translate the sentences into Chinese.

(1) You will find a list of the damaged and missing articles attached.

(2) The machine we bought from you does not perform well.

(3) The shipment delivered does not conform to our contract.

(4) Our customer called us yesterday that the weaving machine we order with you has broken down twice last week, and demanded that the machine be fixed by next weekend.

(5) The delay may be caused by the shipping company.

(6) Please make sure that the goods will be delivered within 7 days, otherwise we will cancel the order and hold you liable for our possible losses.

(7) The consignment delivered to our promises consisted of eight cases, two of which were found broken.

(8) There were also a lot of missing parts mentioned in the manual but which were not in the

box with the item.

(9) We estimate the loss on invoice value to be £ 2,000 for which we claim compensation.

(10) We will be seeking compensation for the delay in delivery according to the contract.

(11) Our conference is scheduled for March 3. With our advance payment, you agreed to have the work completed one week prior to the opening of our conference (a copy of the contract is enclosed).

(12) If the work is not completed by the end of the month, it will be viewed as a breach of the contract, and we will take immediate measures to protect ourselves.

(13) According to the contract, late delivery will result in a penalty of $20 per day.

(14) I ask for replacements for the ceramic flower pots I received, and a refund for the shipping cost of returning the faulty ones to you.

(15) Unless I hear from you within 7 days, I will have to take court action, and the costs of this action will be added to my claim.

4. Can you write a letter of complaint according to the details below?

> May 20, order for 30 coffee assembly kits, paid in advance, delivery, one week overdue, send the items within 7 days, a breach of the contractor, refund the full purchase price

Did you explain what went wrong?
Did you suggest any solution to the problem?
Did you remain polite while compalining?

You can move on to Unit Twelve if you can complete the exercises satisfactorily.

Unit Twelve
Adjustments

An adjustment is the receiver's response to the complaint/claim made by the customer. Customer satisfaction is the top priority for any business wishing to achieve long-term success. Business establishments would give prime importance to customer satisfaction. If there are any issues, they would be ready for an amicable solution.

Responsibility for the problem, reliability of the customer, and the nature of the business relationship are all considered to determine a fair adjustment. While settlements of the customers' requests are done within the bounds of company policy, adjustments strive to restore the customer's goodwill and confidence in the organization. A reply to a complaint/claim must be sent promptly, emphasizing the solution rather than the error, and convincing the customer you understand and want to be fair.

You should treat with respect the customers who file complaints or/and claims. If you handle the situation well, your customer is likely to be even more loyal than before because you have proven that you are serious about customer satisfaction.

Replies to complaint letters must be handled carefully, especially when the requested compensation cannot be granted.

Unit Objectives

After learning the unit, students should be able to handle complaints effectively by:
1. Following the right procedure;
2. Acknowledging the request of the buyer;
3. Explaining the causes of the problem;
4. Offering proper solution;
5. Rejecting claims.

Structure & Content

Complaints fall into two categories: justified complaints and unjustified complaints. In the latter case, you acknowledge that a problem occurred but make it clear that you are not at fault. Be as specific as possible about where the problem lies, and offer to help where you can.

❖ Responses to Unjustified Complaints

Most unjustified complaints do not actually warrant an apology; in fact, apologizing to the customer makes it seem like you should've provided a service where you did not. However, in handling unjustified complaints, you should be polite and restrained. Remember that anyone can make a mistake.

Example One Reply to an unjustified complaint

> Dear Mr. Anderson,
>
> Thank you for your letter dated 16th October 2020. We are sorry to learn the propeller of your motor breaks down.
>
> All our products are backed by a three-year warranty. From the photos and information you forwarded to us it can be concluded that your motor is more than four years old. We are not responsible for any products that are not under warranty.
>
> However, we do however carry a wide variety of reasonably priced universal propellers, one of which I am sure will suit your needs. Please call in at the store so we can help you get back out on the water soon.
>
> Sincerely yours,
>
> Tim Longman

Acknowledging receipt of the complaint

Explaining you are not responsible

Offering to help

Example Two Reply to an unjustified complaint

> Dear Ms. Lyon,
>
> Thank you for your letter of April 25 concerning the goods you ordered 5 weeks ago.
>
> Unless domestic orders for which we guarantee overnight delivery, international orders take at least 4 weeks for delivery, which is stated in the order instructions on our catalog (p.10). As you will see, shipments for London, England usually take 4 weeks.

Referring to the background

Explaining the problem
Implying the complaint is unjustified

> *If you desire faster delivery for your next order, we can send the goods by express delivery. The rate, however, will be considerably higher.*
>
> *Sincerely yours,*
>
> *Li Chen*

Offering other options to help

❖ Response to Justified Complaints

Example Three Reply to a justified complaint

> Dear Ms. Middleton,
>
> Three replacements are on their way to you, freight paid.
>
> When we learnt this morning that three of the eight Canon cameras shipped to you arrived in a damaged condition, we looked into the matter immediately. Our investigation reveals that all the cameras were in satisfactory condition when loaded onto the delivery trucks. Attached you will see a copy of the quality control reports from our dispatch department. It appears that the damage must have occurred during transport and delivery. We will be working with our carrier to determine where and how the damage occurred and take measures to avoid similar mistakes.
>
> Thank you for bringing the matter to our attention, and we look forward to your oncoming orders.
>
> Kind regards,
>
> William Willy

Solution

Background introduction

Explanation

Appreciation

If you agree that the complaint is justified (even if only in part), say so, apologize for the inconveniences caused, provide an explanation and express your desire to correct the problem.

When granting an adjustment, be cheerful, freely admit errors and willingly offer the adjustment. You may also take the opportunity to express appreciation for the information provided, point out that similar errors won't happen again, and suggest future business cooperation.

The typical parts of a letter of adjustment include acknowledgment of the complaint, expression of apology or sympathy, explanations of the problem, and rectification of the complaint, though the rectification sometimes appears at the beginning of the letter.

❖ Acknowledging Receipt of the Complaint

Begin adjustment letters with a positive statement.

This letter is to inform you that we have received your complaint about your June statement.

This is in reference to your complaint dated 15th January 2020.

Thank you for your letter of April 25 concerning the goods you ordered 5 weeks ago.

Thank you for writing us about your irritation concerning the delay in your receipt of the five photocopiers you ordered.

Thank you for your letter of April 25 concerning the carpets you ordered with us on April 3.

Thank you for your letter of 5 August in which you pointed out that three mistakes totaling $337.00 had been made on your statement.

Thank you very much for your order of March 11 for the color TV sets we offered at cost price.

Thank you for your letter of 20 June concerning your order (No. JL0126), which should have been delivered to you on 3 June.

We agree that the usual high standards of our products were not met in this instance.

❖ Apologizing for the Inconveniences Caused

Express your sympathy and understanding.

I apologize for the errors.

We are very sorry that three bicycles arrived broken.

We are sorry that you were not satisfied with your purchase of the bicycles.

First, let me apologize for your order not being delivered on the due date.

We apologize for your order being not only late but also incorrect.

We would like to apologize for the mistake on invoice No.5573, which was due to an oversight.

We take these issues very sincerely and sympathize for the inconvenience caused to you.

❖ Offering an Explanation or/ and a Solution

Offer an explanation and let the reader know what is being done.

In the meantime, we would like to replace your bicycle with a brand new bicycle of the same brand with no shipping costs to you.

We have dispatched 100 new garments by SF Express. They should arrive by 1 February 2021.

I've sent the correct items via China Post (tracking number 001927219777). If you'd like to track the package, please refer to the number.

I have deducted a total of $160.00 from your statement and will send you a new draft for $27,820.6.

We have got the replacements ready for shipment and will dispatch them this afternoon.

To prevent re-occurrences we have set up a verification procedure.

To show our goodwill, we would like to offer you a 5% discount on your next order with us.

Our factory has now inspected the unit you returned last week, and they inform us that the circuits were overloaded. We can repair the machine, but it will be necessary to charge you as incorrect use of the unit is not covered by our guarantee.

While I sympathize with your plight, you did buy the backpack during our two-day Thanksgiving Blowout Sale. Signs posted during the sale said that we could offer no refunds or exchanges. This is the only way that Beds & Beyond can continue to bring you such low prices on our blowout sales.

❖ Ending with a Positive Statement

There will be no such a repetition in the future.

I apologize for the oversight and look forward to your next orders.

Thank you for bringing the matter to our attention and giving us the opportunity to serve. We look forward to your continued patronage.

We value your business and good will and hope you will continue to consult us for your outdoor supplies.

I hope the replacements rushed to you will arrive in time for your building project.

We will make every effort to see that this never happens again.

We assure you that this will not happen again.

I'll follow up to make sure you receive the correct items on time. If you have any questions in the meantime, feel free to contact me directly.

We look forward to receiving your further orders and assure you that they will be fulfilled correctly.

Thank you for your understanding in the matter.

❖ Offering a Compromise

If the situation justifies a compromise, you can use it in making the refusal positive. More specifically, by saying what you can do (the compromise) you can clearly imply what you cannot do.

Please find enclosed a $10.00 gift voucher in appreciation of your custom.

We have enclosed a $100 voucher, with which you can get the nice coat cleaned and ironed.

I am enclosing a $5.00 gift certificate you can redeem at any Walmart store. It is good on all merchandise, including sale items.

Customer satisfaction is very important to us. We are willing to offer you a special 20% discount on all your future purchases.

Expressions to Learn and Remember

Terms to remember

account	credit your account
apology	owe you our apologies, extend my apologies for the inconvenience, accept my sincere apologies
appreciation	appreciate your difficulties, appreciate your patience, appreciate your business
complaint	make complaints, handle complaints, complaint on the defect, justified complaints, unjustified complaints
damage	damage caused by poor packaging, calling our attention to the damage, damage resulting from insufficient packing
delivery	delayed delivery, delays in delivery, deliver goods well in advance of the promised delivery date, ensure punctual delivery
goods	exchange the goods, return the goods with the receipt, replace the goods
order	send the wrong order ordering from an out-of-date catalogue
quality	defective products, faulty merchandize, replace the faulty item without charge
refund	give a full refund, refund you the 10%
replacement	send replacement, provide replacement, ask for a replacement for
solution	discuss a satisfactory solution

Sentence Patterns for Application

Granting requests

1. Seven carefully packed replacement lamps have been dispatched and should reach your sales floor in time for your Saturday promotion.
2. A new consignment of Speedy Mixers was sent to you by air this morning. You will get them within two days.
3. We are arranging to send a fresh consignment of your order within a day or two.
4. The replacement fabric will be sent to you soon.

5. We have checked our accounts and find that we have been sending you the wrong statement due to a confusion in names and addresses.
6. Thank you for calling our attention to the problem. We will be happy to replace the defective machines.
7. Please would you return the whole consignment to us, postage and packing forward, and we will ask the shipping company to inspect the damage so that they can arrange compensation.
8. I have pleasure in enclosing a check for ￥1680. This is due to a miscalculation on our invoice dated 6 March.
9. Please find enclosed our credit note No. c4 for €t65.60 which is a refund for the overcharge on invoice No. 85463. As you pointed out in your letter, the trade discount should have been 25%, not 22%, of the gross price.

Rejecting claims and adjustments

1. We have closely compared the articles you returned with our samples and can see no difference between them.
2. The original receipt of purchase is needed for a full refund.
3. All products returned for refund/replacement or extended on credit must be returned in "saleable" condition with original packing.
4. We are not willing either to substitute the articles or to offer a credit.
5. Upon inspecting the damage to the headset returned, we discovered it results from an accident. We provide replacement for items that have not met our stringent standards, but cannot do so for those damaged by customers. The best we can do is fix the headset at the usual rate.
6. The items on sale cannot be returned, exchanged or refunded. This is the only way that we can continue to bring you such low prices.
7. The warranty covers defects that arise in normal use, but not from abuse.
8. The warranty on the workmanship expired one year ago.
9. From the photos and information you forwarded to us it can be concluded that your motor is more than four years old and it is no longer under warranty.
10. We have received your claims form No. 34276 in which you claimed ￥2,400.00 for damage to your property in your premises. Your policy with us states that you are covered for flooding caused by rain or storms, and not burst water pipes within the premises.
11. We'll certainly stick with your project and address the problem in whatever way you decide on. However, since the mistake is not ours, you'll need to pay for any changes in the original plans.

Samples for Comprehension

❖ Sample One Reply to Unjustified Complaint of Late Delivery

Dear Mr. Green,

Thank you for writing us about your irritation concerning the delay in your receipt of the computers you ordered with us last month.

The delay, however, was not caused at our end. Following the terms specified in your Purchase Order, we shipped the goods via China Post before May 10. As you can see from the attached screenshot of the logistics information, the consignment was picked up by China Post on May 6.

Unless I have misunderstood something, it appears that China Post is responsible for the delay.

Please let me know if I may help further in this matter.

Sincerely,

Mike Reed

Daily Articles Division

❖ Sample Two Reply to Wrong Demand for Payment

Dear Mr. Rick,

We apologize for the billing statement sent to you twice this month. Please disregard the second bill you received.

The mistake on our part was caused by a software malfunction of our accounting system, which has been fixed by now. There will be no such a repetition in the future.

Thank you very much for bringing the matter to our attention and helping us keep transactions systematic.

Thank you for your patience and understanding.

Best regards,

Kate Middleman

Accounting Manager

❖ Sample Three Reply to Unjustified Complaint of Wrong Delivery

Dear Mr. Silver,

Thank you for your letter of 1 June in which you said that you had received a wrong delivery to your order (No.4183).

I have looked into this and found that you have ordered from an out-of-date catalogue. The paint you wanted is listed under GR5678 in the current catalogue.

We will send you the replacement tomorrow and pick up the other consignment at the same time. Meanwhile with the delivery I will include a debit note of $160, which is the difference of the two paints.

A current catalogue is on its way to you in case the one I originally sent you is mislaid.

Yours sincerely,

Jeff Hughes

❖ Sample Four Reply to Late Delivery

Dear Mr. Shakti Ramkumar,

Thank you for your order, which should have reached you by the end of last week. The delay was caused by the snow storms in Northeast of China, which you might have read in *China Daily*. You can expect to receive the items as soon as the weather clears.

I apologize for the inconvenience the delay has caused you. But I am sure you understand that it is beyond our control.

But if you cannot wait, give us a call at our customer service department at 0451-68835102, or e-mail us at sales@wuyingstationery. We will cancel your order and give you a full refund.

Sincerely yours,

Ming Liang

❖ Sample Five Reply to Short Shipment

Dear Mr. Fred Flintstone,

I am sorry for the short shipment we sent you. Upon enquiry, we found that it is a mistake on our part. Your purchase order clearly stated 60 cases, not 30 cases.

We apologize for the mistake and meanwhile there are two options available at this time: we will ship you another 30 cases within the week, or issue you a credit note to adjust the account. Please let me know your preference.

We will do everything we can to ensure that this type of error does not occur again.

Thank you for your understanding.

Sincerely,

Kenneth Beare
Director of Ken's Cheese House

Tasks to Fulfill

scan for the keys

1. Can you answer the questions?

(1) What are the two categories of complaints?
(2) Should you apologize when receiving unjustified complaints?
(3) What is the main content of a reply to justified complaints?
(4) What are the typical parts of a letter of adjustment?

2. Read and answer the following questions.

Dear Mr. Hall,

Thank you for your email on April 25 reporting that one carton of towels is missing.

When we handed the towels to the carrier, we made sure that all 10 cartons were included in the parcel. We will contact our carrier and try to locate the carton and forward it to you as soon as possible. If, in two weeks, we fail to locate it, we will forward a check to you to the value of the missing towels.

We are sorry for the loss and the inconvenience this has caused you.

Thank you for your patience.

Sincerely yours,

Kevin Lucas

Questions:

(1) How did Mr. Hall inform Mr. Lucas of the loss?
(2) How many cartons were packed in the parcel originally?
(3) What will Mr. Lucas do?
(4) What if Mr. Lucas cannot find the lost items in two weeks?
(5) Which words in the letter have a similar meaning to the following?
   A. transport   B. find   C. send

3. Fill in the blanks to complete the letter.

Dear Mr. Smith,

We were sorry to hear that you have not received the computers ordered two months ago. However, (1)_____ (这问题不是我们造成的). We believe the responsibility for the late delivery lies with (2)_____ (物流公司), as we dispatched the goods within the time stipulated in the contract.

I understand (3)_____ (这件事很令人恼火) and I will be happy to help you if I can. We value your business and (4)_____ (期望未来继续与您合作). If you still have further concerns, feel free to (5)_____ (发邮件或者致电) 310-965678.

Regards,

Self-evaluation

1. Can you translate the following expressions into English?

(1) 投诉
(2) 引起不便
(3) 让顾客满足
(4) 引起我们的关注
(5) 为此错误向您道歉
(6) 计算错误
(7) 被计价两次
(8) 退款
(9) 一张 20 美元的礼品券
(10) 处于保修期
(11) 不正常使用造成的损坏
(12) 错发的货物
(13) 维修中心
(14) 按常价修理机器
(15) 修复机器至其完好状态
(16) 满足顾客要求
(17) 提一个折中方案
(18) 退换货物
(19) 邮费
(20) 不可预知的情况

2. Please translate the sentences into English.

(1) 很遗憾您对购买的纯棉床单不满意。
(2) 虽然我们尽力包装好货物，但不幸的是，偶尔也会有货物破损。
(3) 对不起，给您造成了麻烦。信中附有我们的退款单一份。
(4) 谢谢您让我们关注些事。本周内给您交付新货，以取代那些有故障的机器。
(5) 谢谢您来信告知我方 2 月 11 日运送的货物与合同不符。
(6) 我们的司机师傅明天把新货给您送去并取回损坏的物品。
(7) 这些红木工艺品都是我们的工匠手工制成，有时候成品与样品不能完全一致。
(8) 请您把日期延长至 3 月 5 日，以便我们能交付与我们的合约相符的产品，改正我们的错误。

(9) 我们认为差异在合理范围之内，因此无法退款。

(10) 按您的要求，两吨新货今早离开了码头，预计 4 月 6 号抵达你处。

(11) 我们将展开调查，最迟在 12 月 1 日答复您。

(12) 感谢您耐心等待我们处理。

(13) 对不起，这是我方无心之错，是由于生产装配线故障所致。

(14) 对此次意外我们表示抱歉，真诚希望您继续惠顾。

(15) 谢谢您花费时间引起我们对此事的关注，希望您以后继续惠顾。

Did you make any grammar mistake?

Did you make any spelling mistake?

Did you apply the correct business words and adopt proper patterns in your sentences?

3. Please translate the sentences into Chinese.

(1) I apologize for the inconvenience that it has caused you.

(2) We appreciate your business with us.

(3) You can expect the full reimbursement within 2 weeks.

(4) Breakage of this sort does unavoidably occur in cross-country shipping.

(5) I think these delays may have something to do with the haulage contractors.

(6) Your request for the $2400 adjustment on the damage is granted, and the amount will be credited to you June statement.

(7) Please keep the damaged crates in the same condition in which you received them until one of our representatives can inspect them.

(8) I think you agree that this unfortunate accident is a rare exception, and I hope it will not keep you from having merchandise shipped by China Post in the future.

(9) As per your request, our service technicians will call on your clients to repair the malfunctioning machines and troubleshoot all the other machines to avoid future problems.

(10) Since we did everything we could to keep you updated on this new rule, I am sorry to inform you that we cannot issue a reimbursement for the service fee.

(11) From our previous transactions you will realize that this sort of problem is quite unusual. Nevertheless, we are sorry about the inconvenience it has caused you.

(12) Please would you return the whole consignment to us, postage and packing forward, and we will ask the shipping company to inspect the damage so that they can arrange compensation.

(13) The contract has a standard clause stating that delivery dates would be met unless

unforeseen circumstances arose.

(14) We understand your problem and will allow you to cancel your contract, but we will not accept responsibility for any action your customers may take against you.

(15) Please find enclosed a check for $65.6 which is a refund for the overcharge on invoice No. H7496.

4. Can you write a reply to a complaint according to the details below?

> apologize for this delay, caused much inconvenience, the substitute worker misplaced the order, reach you within 3 days, offer a 5% special discount on this order, credit the account accordingly

Did you thank the customer for writing to you?
Did you apologize for the mistake?
Did you point out how you would like to put the matter right?

You can move on to Unit Thirteen if you can complete the exercises satisfactorily.

Unit Thirteen
Agent & Agency

An agent, in legal terminology, is a person who has been legally empowered to act on behalf of another person or an entity. A company can be an agent because a company or organization can be understood in figurative terms as an actor. It has entity status even though it is intangible, a group or association of individuals. An agent may be authorized to represent a client in negotiations and other dealings with third parties or may have decision-making authority. An agency refers to the action or performance of the agent to produce an effect or result. It never denotes an individual.

People hire agents to perform tasks that they lack the time or expertise to do for themselves. Investors hire stockbrokers to act as middlemen between them and the stock market. Athletes and actors hire agents to negotiate contracts on their behalf because the agents are typically more familiar with industry norms and have a better idea of how to position their clients. More commonly, prospective homeowners use agents as middlemen, relying on the professional's greater skills at negotiation. Import and export agents are firms (or individuals) that undertake most of the importing and exporting activities on behalf of their principals usually for a commission. Their primary responsibilities include ensuring secured transportation of goods, making and collecting payments on behalf of customers and dealing with third parties.

Basically, import/export agents link up buyers and sellers, negotiate a deal and get paid for their services. They are similar to distributors in that they are middlemen. However, an agent does not take title to the goods and provides fewer services than a distributor does. The agent's role is to get orders and (usually) earn a commission for his services.

An export agent is a firm (or individual) that undertakes most of the exporting activities on behalf of an exporter usually for a commission. A key feature of the traditional export agent is that they never really take ownership of the goods, which always remain under the control of the exporter.

The choice of an agent in a foreign country is a delicate task, and suppliers should include the following questions in their considerations:
1. What is the company's history and what are the qualifications and backgrounds of the

principal officers?

2. Does the company have adequate trained personnel, facilities, resources to devote to your business?

3. What is their current sales volume?

4. What is the size of their inventory?

5. How will they market your product (retail, wholesale or direct)?

6. Which territories or areas of the country do they cover?

7. Do they have other foreign clients? Are any of these clients your competitors? It is important to obtain references from several current clients?

8. What types of customers do they serve?

9. Do they publish a catalogue?

10. What is their sales force?

If you feel comfortable about the answers to the above question, you may go on to obtain a credit report about their financial positions.

Unit Objectives

After learning the unit, when looking for agents and negotiating agencies, students should be able to:

1. Know what information should be included in considerations of agent and agency;
2. Understand the related business concepts;
3. Adopt proper words, phrases and sentence patterns for such tasks.

Structure & Content

❖ Finding an Agent

As an exporter, finding buyers for your product can be the most difficult challenge in your business, particularly when you're just getting started or are selling in a new market. With different cultural norms, languages, and travel barriers, selling in another country a challenging task. It is never easy.

The exporter can enter the export market by way of trading companies in the foreign country, state-sponsored or state-controlled companies, which import products, usually in bulk orders, buying agents, foreign wholesale distributors——usually private firms, commission agents, and your own salesperson who find individuals and firms for your exports.

Using an agent is a relatively easy way for a local company to enter a foreign market, as the agent does all (or at least some) of the export marketing on the firm's behalf. The agent may travel abroad, do research, prepare an export plan, advise the exporter on how to adapt their marketing mix, make contact with potential buyers, negotiate deals with the buyers, take care of all promotional activities, handle the logistics and documentation, and much more. All of these tasks, the export agent will do on the exporter's behalf.

It is possible to find an agent through the internet, or by advertising. Other methods include contacting government department of trade in your own country or the country you wish to export to, or consulting trade associations.

Once you find an agent, you are to start from a self-introduction, then tell the reader what you want. It is customary that you take the opportunity to convince the agent that the products you make are worth handling and will sell in their market. You close the correspondence by saying that you would be grateful for any help.

❖ Introducing Yourself

We are a professional trader of office paper with a history of more than 30 years.

We are one of the leading producers of children clothing with aggressive growth.

We are a large manufacturing company specializing in high-quality raw peat and peat substrates to help all types of growers reach the best results to their plants.

We are Chinese Industrial Chemicals and Petro Chemicals, and we offer a large variety of chemicals like industrial water treatment, flue gas desulfurization treatment and environment governance treatment.

We are producer of fashion, textile and leather items for leading designers in Israel with service providers around the world and thousands of items produced every month.

We are Bank of China, one of the four major commercial banks in China, with our headquarters in Beijing and branches in many countries.

We are one of the manufacturers of baby care products like silicone feeding bottle, milk warmer, steamer and sterilizer in Shenzhen, China.

We are a Singapore based food distributor dealing in rice, pulses, spices etc. The Company's principal activity is wholesale trade of a variety of goods, supplying to supermarkets as the secondary activity.

❖ Stating What You Want

We are looking to appoint Distributors for our products in South Africa.

Right now we are actively looking for valuable distribution partners/ agents abroad and one of our target zones is North America.

We are a US based manufacturer of premium faucets and accessories for the bathroom. We are searching for a professional sales agent within the Mumbai area who has contacts to bathroom dealers and showrooms as well as to architects and designers.

We are looking for wholesale distributors for our products in Canada.

We are looking to buy electrical heaters of various designs from China.

❖ Convincing the Agent Your Products are Worth Handling and Will Sell Well in Their Market

We offer a wide range of well-designed products which are hardwearing, light, easy to use, and fully guaranteed for one year.

Our prices are extremely competitive for a product of this quality.

Our research shows us that there is a growing demand for this product in your country, and we are sure that once our brand is established it will become a market-leader.

Our fitness supplements are the result of many years' research and development, and we are confident that they will quickly overtake sales of the competing brands at present available in the Swedish market.

We have established an ethical and reliable operation and committed to sourcing and supplying the best quality products.

Founded in 1985, we make machinery for the washing and dyeing of finished garments. Our constant efforts have resulted in a large variety of machines that are high in quality and competitive in price.

We are one of the world's foremost specialists in Bluetooth and mobile telecommunications accessories, with an established global reputation for delivering sleek, ergonomic products at outstanding value (see more at our website).

❖ Closing

Thank you in advance for your help.

We hope you can help us, and look forward to hearing from you.

We look forward to receiving your recommendation.

Interested parties please contact us quickly. Thank you.

Please contact us if you are interested in our products.

If you are interested please contact us via email.

We are looking forward to getting your response as soon as possible.

❖ Asking for An Agency

If an individual or organization intends to act as a supplier's agent, they can contact the supplier directly or advertising their agency. Like suppliers who are looking for agents, they also start by stating who they are, what they want, and then convince the readers before bringing their request to an end.

❖ Introducing Yourself

We are wholesaler and retailer of beauty products. We are leading independent importer and distributor of fresh produce in the UK.

Our company is a Commercial Agency based in northern Greece, dealing with Greek Factories Packers/Exporters of canned Peaches, extra virgin Olive Oil, Table Olives and Fruit Puree (mainly from Peaches and Apricots).

Founded in 1979, our business includes the wholesale distribution of jewelry, precious stones and metals, costume jewelry, watches, clocks, and silverware.

We are distributors of Industrial automation spare parts in the middle east for the last 5 years.
We are a well-established importer and distributor of food products, importing food products from different countries and distributing to all wholesale buyers, retails shops and super markets throughout the entire European Union countries. We have been in this business since 2005.

We are sourcing and buying agency in Canada, dealing with wholesale of lifestyle products on a B2B platform and also have an e-commerce platform to sell B2C.

We are sourcing and buying agency(采购代理).

❖ Stating What You Want

We would like to buy De-Husked Coconuts in bulk quantity.

We are looking forward to expanding our business and interested in being Agent/Distributor for Food Products/Edible Oil.

Presently, we are in search of suppliers of various tea, such as green tea, black tea, loose tea, tea cake, etc. We would be grateful if you could email us your best FOB price with expected delivery time along with your product catalog.

We would be interested to learn more about your products and understand further if we could collaborate on promoting and marketing your products in the North American market.

We would like to work as an Agent/Distributor of wooden products and crafts.

We are looking for importers in the UK who would be interested in representing/ reselling our chemical products under an exclusive distribution agreement. Growers, nurseries, tenders, and all other categories are welcome to contact us.

❖ Convincing/Suggesting

We have all the required infrastructure.

We have been in this business since 1985.

With our infrastructure, sales team, and other resources, we can offer you first-class representation and excellent sale.

Through a huge wide network of clients and contacts, we manage to market different products according to market needs.

We are ready to provide all business resources and investment will be done as per the requirement of the company.

We have a network of branded customers like Disney and HaiDiLao.

In the last 12 months we have significantly grown our network of agents and distributors, with nearly all continents now covered by at least one representative.

We are committed to providing the highest levels of quality and service to our clients.

We can offer you first-class representation and excellent sales, and guarantee the success of your products in this country.

At the moment we would like to expand our business and work as a sole Agent/Distributor of Costume Jewelry in East Africa. We are ready to provide business.

We are Bank of China and are looking for partners in Hong Kong who would be interested to represent us there.

❖ Suggesting Business Terms

Delivery should be made within six weeks from receipt of order.

We operate on a 10% commission basis on net list prices.

Our customers usually settle with us direct, and we pay our principals by bill of exchange on a quarterly basis.

With regard to payments, we suggest customers settle with us direct, and we then remit quarterly account sales deducting our commission.

We can hold stock if necessary.

We would expect your help with advertising.

Payment is to be made by letter of credit.

For disagreement, if any, over the terms of the contract, we would like to refer to US Commerce in arbitration.

If these conditions are acceptable, then we would be pleased take on an initial one-year contract to act as your agents.

❖ Encouraging Further Contacts

Please contact us for long term business.

Please contact us for long term profitable business. Please visit our website for more products.

Please have a look at our website to know more. We hope to hear from you soon.

We would be interested to learn more about your products and understand further if we could collaborate on promoting and marketing your products in the North American market.

Electrolube is particularly interested to hear from anyone in Eastern Europe, Scandinavia, Asia, South America or North America. For more information, please contact our office in the UK on +44 19520530.

If you are interested in working with us then, please send your products catalog, pricing, company profile etc. for further discussion.

Expressions to Learn and Remember

Terms to remember

Agent	buying agents
Agency	import-export agency, do business on the agency's behalf
Commission	earn a commission on any sales generated
Distributor	appoint distributor, seek distributor, look for distributor
Manufacturer	a well-established manufacturer, manufacturer of office paper, professional manufacturer of

Sentence Patterns for Application

Introducing yourself

1. We are a Europe based reputed pharmaceutical company.
2. We are a global leader in wood cutting machine industry.
3. Our company specializes in medicines intended for animals and humans in West Africa and Asia.
4. Ours is the pharmaceutical division of International Corporations in the UK, which is based in Belgium.
5. You probably associate our name with the manufacture of chemicals / textiles /machines /furniture.
6. We are leader in manufacturing electrical and electronic products in China, and we are looking for local distributors/sales agents who can help us to sell our products to the Indian market.
7. We specialize in producing car paint, with an annual production of 200,000 tons.
8. Established in 1992, we are one of the leading professional battery manufacturers in China.
9. We are an Australian certified coffee and tea company, exercising in manufacturing hot brews for cafe and home.

Stressing strong points

1. Our wide range of wood cutting machines is hardwearing, light, easy to use, and fully guaranteed for one year.
2. Our daily apparel and underwear products are high in quality, low in price and beautiful in design.
3. Our prices are extremely competitive for a product of this quality.
4. We have learnt that there is a growing demand for this product in your country, and we are sure they will sell well and become a market-leader.
5. Our confidence in the products is supported by many years' research and development.
6. We have established an ethical and reliable operation and committed to sourcing and supplying the best quality products.
7. Our trouble-free cleaners will quickly overtake sales of the competing brands at present available in the European market.
8. We enjoy a worldwide reputation as a reliable supplier for high quality goods, prompt delivery and first, class after sale service.
9. With our infrastructure, sales team and other resources, we can offer you first-class representation and excellent sale.
10. Founded in 1985, we make machinery for the washing and dyeing of finished garments. Our constant efforts have resulted in a large variety of machines that are high in quality and competitive in price.
11. We have a warehouse and a distribution center in Shanghai, which handles food and beverage wholesale distribution and outlets in more than 30 cities in China. We have long-term business relationship with supermarkets, restaurants, clubs, taverns, hotels, motels and liquor stores.

Inviting agents

1. We are looking for distributors across Europe who are familiar with the local market.
2. We have the necessary documents and are interested to do business with individuals or companies who would like to sell the products on our behalf in the regions mentioned above.
3. We are looking for an importer and distributor of pharmaceutical ingredients and cosmetic items. Details will be sent on receipt of any instructions.

4. Electrolube's international network is growing fast, and we're now actively seeking other companies who want to be a part of it. The agent we are looking for must have proper infrastructure to distribute.
5. We are looking for a sole agent who will sell and distribute our products with high fee commission in Japan.
6. Professionals with sales experiences in areas such as elevators / machine tools / compressors are preferred.
7. We would like to appoint Distributors Medical Sterilization in new territories to replicate the success we have with our current partners around the world. Contact us for further details.
8. We are looking forward to expanding our business and interested in being Agent/ Distributor for Food Products/Edible Oil.
9. Presently, we are in search of suppliers of wood incense in different shapes like cubes, sticks, cones, etc. from Asia.
10. We are looking for trading companies in South Africa that can represent/ resell our stainless kitchenware.

Stating business terms and conditions

1. We expect a 10% commission on net list prices.
2. The distributors we want to appoint will buy our products on their own account and then retail them at market prices in their country.
3. We offer a 30% trade discount off net list prices and a further 5% quantity discount for sales above $100,000
4. We offer a 5% commission on CIF invoice values, and we deliver within 5 weeks of receipt of international orders.
5. The bulk orders we place with you will be paid by L/C after shipping.
6. We would like to conclude our transactions on an FOB basis, with a 25% trade discount on net invoice values.
7. Our customers will settle with us direct, and we pay our suppliers by monthly statements.
8. We will be highly obliged if you could email us best FOB price with expected delivery time along with your product catalog.

Samples for Comprehension

❖ Sample One Looking for a Commission Agent

Dear Sir or Madam,

We are a large manufacturing company based in Yingkou, Liaoning, China. We specialize in chemical products. We are trying to find an established firm to represent us in selling our products in Europe, especially in Germany. At present we are exporting to Vietnam, India and some African countries, but we would like to expand our business to the European market.

The agency we are offering will be on a commission basis, and as we are eager to get into the European market, we are prepared to offer a 15% commission to our agents, plus a substantial advertising allowance.

Please find enclosed our current brochure which can give you details of our company.

We hope you can help us, and look forward to hearing from you soon.

Yours faithfully,

Liu Hui

❖ Sample Two Looking for a Sole Agent

Dear Sir or Madam,

You probably associate our name with the manufacturer of textiles in China. We would like to appoint a sole agent in your country to act on our behalf selling silk and cotton products. As you can see from the enclosed catalog, we can offer a wide selection of products which are attractive in design, high in quality and competitive in price. And we have noticed that there is a growing demand for our products in your country and we are sure that once they are put on your market, they will enjoy a ready sale.

As an inducement to the agent we appoint, we will be offering a 15% commission on net prices.

We would be grateful if you could introduce our name to your correspondents in the area and help us to get in touch with some suitable and reliable firms.

Thank you in advance for your help and we look forward to hearing from you soon.

Yours faithfully,

Jane Russel

❖ Sample Three Advertising for an Agent

Dear Sir or Madam,

We are one of the world's foremost specialists in Bluetooth and mobile telecommunications accessories. We have established a firm and global reputation for supplying sleek, ergonomic products at outstanding value (see more at our website). We are inviting distributors to market our bluetooth headsets in Central America.

If you have storage space and investment capacity, please contact us for further discussion.

Faithfully,

Sam Bush

❖ Sample Four Asking for an Agent

Dear Sir or Madam,

We are one of the leading companies in dairy retail business. We are interested in your cheeses displayed at Beijing Agricultural Fair held last year in China, and would like to know whether you could offer us a sole agency to retail your products in China.

We enjoy an established reputation and have outlets throughout China. We are sure that we would be the best company to represent you here and are willing to offer you references.

We expect a sole agency in China, and a 10% commission on net list prices with an additional 3% del credere commission. Our customers usually settle with us direct, and we pay our suppliers by bill of exchange on a quarterly basis.

We can offer you first class representation and excellent sales to guarantee the success of your products in our country. We look forward to hearing that you are interested in our proposal.

Yours faithfully,

Geoerge Bush

❖ Sample Five Offering to be an Agent

Dear Sir or Madam,

We are a leading importer and distributor of food products. We mainly import food products from different countries and distribute to all wholesale buyers, retail shops and super markets. We cover entire European Union countries. Our major products are Rice varieties, frozen foods, Snacks, oil and so on. To know our product range, please visit our homepage.

Presently we are looking for Chinese suppliers who can supply quality powdered flour of rice and wheat.

Please contact us through email with competitive quotations.

Thank you,
Faithfully

Sam Wong

❖ Sample Six Discussing Business Terms

Dear Mr. Kingsbury,

Thank you for offering us a sole agency for your products in Singapore.

We are confident that we can handle the kind of business you described in your letter of 9 May, and we agree with you that the demand for your tires here is increasing. However, there are some points we would like to clarify with you before we make a decision.

1. How would payment be arranged? By bill of exchange, letter of credit, or bank draft?
2. Do you offer support for advertising?
3. If a disagreement arises over the terms of the contract, who would be referred to in arbitration?
4. How long would the initial contract run?

If you can send us a draft contract including all the necessary details, we will give you a more definite reply.

We look forward to hearing from you soon.

Yours sincerely,

Ann Catherine

Tasks to Fulfill

scan for the keys

1. Can you answer the questions?

(1) What is an agent?
(2) Why do people hire agents?
(3) What are some of the concerns in looking for an agent?
(4) How can you convince a supplier you are an ideal agent?

2. Read and answer the following questions.

Dear Mr. Kassie,

Thank you for your email. As you requested, we enclose a draft contract for the agency agreement.

As you will see, you would be required to hold only a representative selection of our products. We can meet orders from the Middle East within four weeks of receipt of orders. Advertising leaflets and brochures would be sent to you in addition to the $2000 in the first year for publicity which could be spent on any type of advertising you think most suitable for your market.

As for terms of payment, we prefer our customers to pay us direct, and usually deal on a letter of credit basis.

The initial contract will be for one year, subject to renewal by mutual agreement.

Disputes, if any, would be settled with reference to EU law.

If you have any further questions with regard to the contract, or anything else, please contact me.

I look forward to hearing from you.

Yours sincerely,

Neek Jay

Belgium Glass

Questions:

(1) What is enclosed in the letter?
(2) How would customers pay Belgium Glass?
(3) What sort of advertising material does Mr. Jay offer?
(4) How long would the agency run initially?
(5) Which words in the letter have a similar meaning to the following?
   A. typical   B. complete   C. first   D. disagreement

3. Fill in the blanks to complete the letter.

Dear Mr. Chauvin,

We are an international (1)_____ (采购公司) based in Hong Kong. We (2)_____ (专营) office facilities. The office paper you advertised on South China Daily interests us, and we would like to work with you (3)_____(以赚取佣金的方式). We have marketing teams in China, USA, EU, UK, and INDIA. At present we represent a number of manufacturers in different countries and regions, but none is from Israel.

We have (4)_____ (拥有所需的一切资源) and more can be arranged as per the requirement.

If you are interested, please send us (5)_____ (你们的产品目录、价格表和公司简介) and tell us how long delivery can be made after receipt of orders from our client.

I look forward to hearing from you soon.

Yours sincerely,

Brtian Ellison

Self-evaluation

1. Can you translate the following Chinese expressions into English?

(1) 代理   (2) 寻求代理   (3) 分销   (4) 供货商
(5) 生产厂家   (6) 出口商   (7) 进口商   (8) 佣金
(9) 总部   (10) 拥有资源和关系   (11) 有销售经验   (12) 网站地址

(13) 专营粮油　　(14) 广告支持　　(15) 年营业额　　(16) 直接付款给我方
(17) 起草合同　　(18) 提供售后服务　(19) 扩大生意至　(20) 签署合同

2. Please translate the sentences into English.

(1) 我方生产各类润滑剂，寻求非洲地区的代理商或分销商。

(2) 我们正在寻找一家当地公司，对作独家代理感兴趣并代表我公司销售我公司的货物和产品。

(3) 我们寻求替我们向独立童装店销售儿童服装的代理，应聘者需有经销童装的经验。

(4) 我们是世界领先的木头加工机械生产厂家，我们的切割机独具特色，操作简单。如果您有兴趣拓展业务与我方合作，请电邮我方贵公司简介。

(5) 我们是以色列独家代理，供应糖尿病人专用的护肤品。我们的产品浓度高，深层保湿效果好，能治疗并保护因糖尿病引起的干燥受损肌肤。

(6) 我们是一家医药公司，总部在广州，正在寻求与医疗产品的生产厂家和供货商之间的合作，以售卖分销他们的医疗产品。

(7) 我们专营蔬菜水果，愿意在南非代销你们的产品。如您感兴趣，请电邮我方你们最新的产品目录、价格单及交易条件。

(8) 我们是香港的一家贸易代理商，寻求与公司合作，售卖公司的电器。我们目前拥有所有需要的资源，并能按照要求提供更多。

(9) 我们寻求中国地区拥有高技术且可靠的生产商，为了未来可能的合作，请把贵厂的网站地址发给我方。

(10) 我们是一家大型摩托车零售连锁店，我们分店遍布英国，我们对贵厂最近在柏林交易会上展出的摩托车很感兴趣。

(11) 我们是一家大的进口代理公司，地处上海并经销工业锅炉。本公司与全中国各地的老牌公司有众多联系，它们对贵公司的产品有需求。

(12) 你会发现代销我们的产品是十分有利可图的，因为我们提供的产品种类繁多，设计美观，质量上乘，价格合理，且提供一流的售后服务和全面保修 2 年。

(13) 作为对我们指定的代理的鼓励，我们愿提供 15% 的佣金，外加相当数额的广告费用。如果销售情况成功，我们将把你的代理范围扩大到全国东部地区。

(14) 我们期望厂家每年给我们额外提供 $50,000 的广告开支，以便我们开展有助于促销产品的广告宣传，还要提供小册子等广告资料。作为回报我们保证年销售 3,000 台摩托车。

(15) 本合同有效期为 1 年，从 10 月 1 日起算。经双方协商同意可再延长一年。如有争议，协商解决。

Did you make any grammar mistake?
Did you make any spelling mistake?

Did you apply the correct business words and adopt proper patterns in your sentences?

3. Please translate the sentences into Chinese.
(1) While your margins may be smaller by selling to a middleman, the time you save trying to sell your exports directly to the market may be well worth it.
(2) Local dealers/distributors interested in our products are being requested to contact us immediately.
(3) We can help arrange transportation and collect payments on behalf of our client.
(4) We are a cosmo-medical company established in Canada in 2003.
(5) We are looking for experienced pharmaceutical and cosmetics agents and distributors in African countries.
(6) If you believe you have the resources to represent us in Africa, and feel that you can develop this market, please contact us as soon as possible.
(7) As you will see from the attached catalogue, we are manufacturers of high quality liquid soaps.
(8) We produce a wide selection of skincare products from cleaning lotions to facial creams.
(9) We are one of the leading marketing firms in Thailand and have successfully represented many products from China, Brazil and the United States.
(10) The type of agency we are looking for will be able to cover the whole of North America.
(11) This is a unique opportunity for someone to start in an expanding market and grow with it.
(12) With regard to payments, we feel it would be preferable for customers to settle with us direct, and we would remit quarterly account sales deducting our commission.
(13) Our organization would offer you first-class representation and excellent sales, and guarantee the success of your products in this country.
(14) The initial contract would be for one year, subject to renewal by mutual agreement.
(15) Disputes, if any, would be settled with reference to Chinese law.

4. Please write to invite interested individuals or companies to act as your agent according to the details below.

> exporter, producer of fashion, textile and leather items, service centers around the world, seek agents/distributors with serious background and connections, 15% commission, advertising allowances, delivery within 6 weeks.

Did you introduce who you are, what you want?
Did you try to convince your prospective agent that it is worthwhile to represent you?
Did you state clearly your business terms and conditions?

You can move on to Unit Fourteen if you can complete the exercises satisfactorily.

Unit Fourteen
Good, Neutral & Bad Messages

Business correspondences, based on their content or messages, fall into three categories: good-news messages, neutral messages and bad-news messages. Those business correspondences that transmit either good news or neutral information are relatively easy to write (Lahiff & Penrose, 1997), as the writer is complying with the wishes of the readers, while a bad-news message is a letter, memo, or email that conveys negative or unpleasant information—information that is likely to disappoint, upset, or even anger a reader.

Good-news, neutral and bad-news messages apply to different situations. Good-news and neutral messages transmit either good news or routine, neutral information. Typical good-news messages include answering inquiries, granting requests for adjustment, approving credit, acknowledging orders, granting favors and other requests, job acceptance letters, and goodwill messages such as appreciation, congratulation, and condolence letters; neutral messages cover announcements about sales and events, procedures, policies, announcing honors and activities of people; and bad-news messages include rejections (in response to job applications, promotion requests, and the like), negative evaluations, and announcements of policy changes that don't benefit the reader.

They follow different organizational patterns.

Unit Objectives

After learning the unit, students should be able to compose business messages effectively by:
1. Identifying the nature of the messages to be composed;
2. Adopting proper organizations for favorable replies and neutral messages;
3. Adopting proper organizations for unfavorable replies;
4. Using proper buffer for bad-news messages.

Structure & Content

A good-news letter begins with the good news.

A neutral letter begins with a message neither good nor bad.

A bad-news letter begins with a buffer.

❖ Good-news and Neutral Messages

Good-news and neutral messages are generally organized by the direct approach. A good-news message begins with the good news and a neutral one begins with a message neither good nor bad. Both writers start with the main idea, then present the secondary details and close on a positive note.

❖ Answering Inquiries

Example One Offering an appointment

> On behalf of UCAR and the NASA Living With a Star Jack Eddy Postdoctoral Fellowship Program, I am pleased to offer you a postdoctoral fellowship, working with Dr. Lyon at UCLA. The appointment will be for one year, and based on continual program funding and satisfactory performance will be renewable for a second year. For the first year you will receive a monthly salary of $6200.00.
>
> The activation of this appointment is contingent on certification by your university that you have been awarded the doctoral degree. Please ask your graduate dean to certify to our office in writing the grading of this degree. In the meantime, you will need to contact Dr. Lyons to determine a mutually acceptable start date. All start dates must fall on a Monday. Please contact my office with this date as soon as it is available. The appointment should commence by December 11, 2020.

Introducing the best news first
Stating the details

Elaborating on secondary details

Example Two Replying to enquiry

> Dear Mr. Moor,
>
> We greatly appreciate your interest in Rainbow Personal Care Products. We have enclosed a catalog of all of our personal care items for your reference.
>
> The baby lotion that you were particularly looking for is listed on Page 7. Our wide selection of skin care items, creams, lotions, soaps, and many others, are safe enough for even the most delicate skin, even for infants. They're all organic, mild, and PH-balanced.

Acknowledging receipt of enquiry & complying with the reader's wishes
Providing detailed information Stressing the selling points

Should you need more information on our products, you can call the customer service department at 1234567, or visit a Rainbow Store near you. Sincerely, *Elon Kean*	Encouraging further contacts

Example Three Granting requests for adjustment

Dear Mrs. Watson,	
Ten carefully packed lawn umbrellas are being shipped prepaid today. They should reach your store in a few days.	Complying with the reader's wishes
Because your satisfaction with our service and products is important to us, we have thoroughly checked our shipping procedures. It appears that the torn umbrellas are the results of insufficient packing. We have taken special care to assure safe arrival of all future shipments.	Explaining the problem
I have enclosed our spring catalogue of lawn furniture and accessories, ranging from small tables to foundations. And you may be interested in our newly-introduced vinyl-coated nylon umbrella, which are superior to the polyester and cotton ones in the market.	Offering opportunity for future cooperation
We apologize for the inconveniences caused. And we promise that there will be no such repetitions in the future. Sincerely yours *Stephanie King*	Apologizing for the inconvenience

❖ Granting Requests

When you say "yes" to a request, granting favor by serving a committee, speaking at a convention, donating money, or lending your firm's equipment without charge, you write to grant the request following the communication patterns below.

Example Four Approving credit

Dear Mr. Rochester,

We are pleased to inform you that your application for credit has been approved. The allowed credit limit for you is $ 60,000, with a monthly interest rate of 1.5% on the total bill. Billing will be done on the 15th of every month.

Please kindly note that the bill must be cleared every six months. Failure to do so will result in double interest rate on the outstanding amount. The bank reserves the right to cancel your current credit and reject future credit requests in case of non-payment for a period of 24 months. Please have a look at the enclosed terms and conditions for more information. For detailed terms and conditions, please refer to the enclosed brochure.

Our customer care is available 24 hours in case you have any queries. Do let us know if you need further assistance.

Complying with the reader's wishes

Explaining terms of the credit facilities

Offering help

The neutral messages transmit either good news or routine messages. They can be unsolicited (主动提出的) messages, such as announcements or transmittals (通知). They are also written to inform the readers of such events as sales, promotions, policies, honors and activities of people, etc.

Example Five Announcing inspections

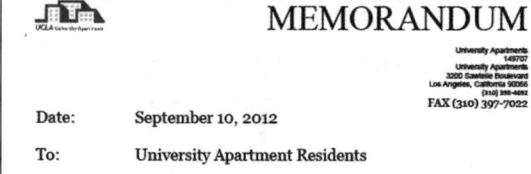

MEMORANDUM

University Apartments
149707
University Apartments
3200 Sawtelle Boulevard
Los Angeles, California 90066
(310) 398-4692
FAX (310) 397-7022

Date: September 10, 2012
To: University Apartment Residents
From: University Apartments Facilities
Re: COMMON AREA HALLWAY CLEANING

If you are receiving this memo, please be informed On **Thursday, September 13, 2012** all of the Common Area Hallway carpeting throughout your building and community will be steamed cleaned.

Work will commence after 8:00 AM and with multiple trucks and personnel Stanley Steemer will complete the cleaning in one day.

Please be aware of the wet floor signs to remind you the hallway carpet will be damp for a couple of hours after the cleaning. Be extra cautious transitioning from the carpeted floors to tile as your shoes may be damp.

If you have any questions related to this matter, please contact UA Facilities at 310.391.4692

The most important message first

Secondary details
Friendly reminder

Clue for further communication

Example Six Announcing water service interruption

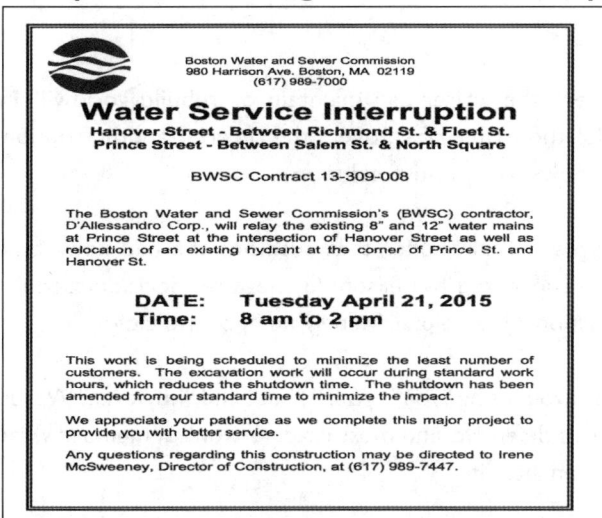

The most important message first

Secondary details

Further explanation
Friendly reminder
Clue for further communication

❖ Bad-news Messages

A bad-news message is a letter, memo, or email that conveys negative or unpleasant information—information that is likely to disappoint, upset, or even anger a reader.

Bad-news messages include rejections (in response to claims, job applications, promotion requests, and the like), negative evaluations, and announcements of policy changes that don't benefit the reader.

Typical examples are collection letters, information of product defects and recalls, declining requests, rejecting claim or adjustment, announcing price increases, etc.

A bad-news message conventionally begins with a neutral or positive buffer statement before introducing the negative or unpleasant information. This approach is called the indirect plan.

You should bear the twofold-purpose in communicating bad news: first, say "no" or to convey bad news, and second, to retain the reader's goodwill.

Bad-news messages are difficult to write.

The first paragraph usually aims to accomplish the following objectives: (1) provide a buffer to cushion the bad news that will follow, (2) let the receiver know what the message is about without stating the obvious, and (3) serve as a transition into the discussion of reasons without revealing the bad news or leading the receiver to expect good news.

The body paragraph(s) deliver the bad news and the reasons for the decision. The bad message, embedded in a supporting, not the topical, sentence of a paragraph is to be stated briefly, clearly and concisely. There is no need to apologize for your decision. There is no reason to apologize for any reasonable business decision.

The closing of a bad-news message is where the writer can maintain or rebuild goodwill. In addition to be sincere, courteous and helpful, the writer often offers the receiver another option, which shifts the emphasis from the negative news to a positive solution.

All in all, the general plan for such messages is (1) A buffer that cushions the bad news that will follow; (2) explanation of your decision supported by reason; (3) negative decision tactfully expressed or understood with helpful suggestion; (4) a helpful, friendly, and positive close.

Besides, in transmitting negative information, avoid using "you" "your" "but" and "however." Words like "you" and "your" could make the receivers defensive, and most readers won't remember what is written before the "but," only what is written after it.

Buffers that reduce the impact of the negative information fall into the following categories: agreement, appreciation, assurance, compliment, cooperation, introduction of the topic and its context, etc.

Agreement
Find a point on which you and the reader share similar views. For example:
We both know how hard it is to make a profit in this industry.

Appreciation
Express sincere thanks for receiving something. For example:
Thank you for choosing us to ship the goods to your client.
We are sincerely grateful for your credit application and will do all that we reasonable can to help you get your business started.

Assurance
We are sure you enjoyed the shipment of books sent last week.

Compliment
Your efforts to build the fund for street dogs are most commendable. We resonably and appreciate the important work your organization does for the poor animals and our environment.

Cooperation
Certainly, you have a right to expect the best possible service from Dell Computer.

Introduction of the topic and its context
Periodically, insurance companies review their policies, assess the cost of offering the policies, and make changes where needed. When that happens, it's my responsibility as an insurance agent to inform my clients and help them make necessary adjustments.

Example Seven

Dear Mr. Silver

Thank you for your interest in the Pharmacy Manager position. Your application and resume were received at our Human Resources office and given careful consideration.

Whilst your application and credentials were impressive, your relative lack of experience was unfortunate. Your resume indicates that you recently graduated from the University of the Pacific, School of Pharmacy, which is below the job criteria that require three-year experience as a pharmacist and a current hawaii state license as a registered pharmacist.

You will no doubt find employment soon but please do not hesitate to apply for any further positions we may advertise.

Sincerely yours,

Oscar Zorn

- Beginning with appreciation
- Revealing the negative information and the reason for the decision
- A friendly and positive close

Example Eight

Dear Mr. Stone

Thank you for your application requesting an extension of your credit for the payment of $10,000 for a duration of three months.

We fully understand your difficulties in settling the account. Nevertheless, it was in consideration of the current economic situation that we have allowed you a grace period of 60 days, which is the best offer we can afford at present. We are also obligated to pay our dues on time.

We sincerely hope that we will continue our mutually beneficial business relationship.

Your Sincerely,

Nora

- Beginning with appreciation
- Delivering the bad message with reasons for the decision
- Expressing goodwill

Example Nine

Dear Ms. King:	
We recognize and appreciate the important work your organization does for the kids in our community through your annual Reading for Better drive.	Compliment
It was a real pleasure for us to contribute some to your drive last year. As much as we would like to continue to support Reading for Better this year, the financial difficulty caused by Covid-19 has prevented us from doing so. Our factory has been closed down for more than three months.	Negative message followed by explanations
We do wish you the best in your endeavors and hope to be able to assist you in the future.	Helpful, friendly, and positive close
Sincerely yours,	
Bush George	

Example Ten

Dear Ms. Jones,	
You may also have noticed the rapid rise in labor and operating costs these days. Although we have tried very hard to keep our prices as low as possible, we are now forced to increase our prices by 5%, effective June 15. You will find enclosed an updated price list. Orders received before that date will be filled at current prices.	Introducing the topic and its context

Revealing the negative message |
We appreciate your understanding and continuing patronage during this market fluctuation. And we trust you agree that in spite of this price adjustment our prices still remain competitive.	Explaining that the price remains competitive in spite of the price change
We value your business and hope to meet your needs for years to come.	Friendly and positive close
Yours sincerely,	
J. Longman	

Example Eleven

Dear Miss Strong:	
We have received your claims form No. 34276 in which you claimed $2,400.00 for damage to your stock of packet goods by flooding in your premises.	Acknowledging receipt of the claim
Policy No. CP 854/341 states that you are covered for flooding caused by rain or storms, and not burst water pipes within the premises.	Reason for rejecting the claim
If you'd like to get a comprehensive policy that can cover you against any eventuality, I would recommend our All Risks policy.	Positive close with a helpful gesture
Yours sincerely,	
Mary Turner	

Sentence Patterns for Application

Agreeing

1. It is a good idea to start a neighborhood reading club.
2. The housing prices are truly rocketing to the sky.
3. I agree that regular training would help your staff be more productive.
4. I agree that a product you purchase should last longer than a few months.
5. We both recognize the promotional possibilities that often accompany a big anniversary sale such as yours.
6. You have every right to be disappointed. I am truly sorry that our product failed to perform as expected.

Appreciating

1. We appreciate that you recognize and value the quality of our produce and service.
2. Thank you for your inquiry regarding employment with Avery Dennison.

3. Thank you for your letter of September 15. We appreciate your inquiry concerning the automatic sprinkler.
4. Thank you for submitting your request for 10 days of vacation in August.
5. Thank you for your check for $945.07 on Invoice No. 226505 which we received today.
6. Thank you for your order. We appreciate your interest in our product and are confident you will love it.

Assuring

1. I am sure you and your guests will find our muffins a tasty addition to your menu.
2. Our appliances will play a role in your success.
3. We do take pride in supplying the finest products at rock-bottom prices.
4. We do offer money-back guarantee, which insures your satisfaction.
5. The olive oil you bought is among the best of its kind.
6. Our policy guarantees a refund of the price difference for 30 days after your purchase.

Complimenting

1. Your efforts to help the homeless seniors are most commendable.
2. We recognize and appreciate your Family First Center's project.
3. Congratulations on the growth of your stores and for your leadership in the Boston market for ten years.
4. Your order for 600 of our air-conditioners suggests you are doing very well.
5. Your regular gift of $25 will help provide essential therapy and equipment to people living with cerebral palsy as well as help our dedicated researchers uncover the very best treatment and interventions.
6. Your invitation for me to act as chairperson for the 11th upcoming Space and Ocean Conference is an honor. I enjoyed serving in that role last year.

Introducing the topic and its context

1. A replacement knob for your range is on its way, shipped February 10 via UPS.
2. As you know, this past Monday, July 12, the FDA came to our plant for a spot inspection. I'm writing to share the inspection results and our response.

3. Yesterday last year's sales report from the Marketing Department came, along with a summary of our customer survey (copies attached).
4. We do pride ourselves on offering our customers the best possible service.
5. I can understand how you felt when you had to pay $168 for the repair.
6. We have just received a donation of baseball jerseys for our little league team from a new business in town. Apparently, the shirts we ordered yesterday are no longer needed.

Samples for Comprehension

❖ Sample One Granting Request for Information

Dear Mr. Jason,

I am replying to your enquiry about the company mentioned in your letter of 30 May.

The company has an excellent reputation in China for both service and the way they conduct their business with their associates in the trade.

We have been dealing with the company for 10 years and allow them credit facilities of up to $5,000. They have always fulfilled their financial obligations to us promptly and satisfactorily. We have never had a problem with them or their accounts.

We take no responsibility as to how the information is used.

Yours sincerely,

Velva Trump

❖ Sample Two Replying to an Advertisement

Dear Mr. Stone,

We are more than happy to submit our proposal and bid for the project you advertised on China Daily on 12 April, 2020. We have attached a document that details the specifics of our proposal, which we feel you will find favorable regarding what you need.

Our company is dedicated to the production of the highest quality of projects with the best service possible to our clients.

We would like to extend our sincerest gratitude for giving us the opportunity to show what we can do for you. We hope to meet with you soon.

Thank you.

Sincerely,

Issac Potter

❖ Sample Three Memo Announcement for Inspection

MEMORANDUM

University Apartments South
3200 Sawtelle Boulevard
Los Angeles, CA 90034

(310) 398-4692

September 10, 2012

To: Keystone/Mentone Residents

From: University Apartments South Facilities Department

Subject: Apartment Entry for HVAC (Heating Units) Inspections
Wednesday, September 12, 2012, 9am-4:30pm

To inspect the HVAC system (Heating Units), UCLA Facilities will need to enter Keystone/Mentone apartments on Wednesday, September 12, 2012, 9 A.M.-4:30 P.M.

Facilities staff will knock first before entering. Please contact Facilities should you have questions or comments regarding this memo, 310-391-0686.

We appreciate your understanding and cooperation.

UA Administrative Offices

❖ Sample Four Refusing Request for Donation

Dear Ms. Ellison:

Your efforts to build the scholarship fund for the association's needy children are most commendable. We wish you good success in your efforts to further this worthy cause.

We at Xiannong are always willing to assist worthy causes whenever we can. That is why every January we budget for the year the maximum amount we believe we are able to contribute to such causes. Then we distribute that amount among the various deserving groups as far as it will go. Since our budgeted contributions for this year have already been made, we are placing your organization on our list for consideration next year.

We wish you success in your efforts to help educate the deserving children of the association's members.

Yours sincerely,

Jane Huang

❖ Sample Five Explaining Travel Information

Important Travel and Meeting Information

To: Meeting Participants for the HSR19 Week 1 Panels (January 7-10, 2020)
FROM: S. Pearl – Meeting Planner, NASA Research & Education Support Services (NRESS)

This document contains travel information regarding your hotel, airline, and other arrangements. As your Meeting Planner for this upcoming event, I am available to answer any travel-related questions at (202) 679-9030 Ext. 231 or spearl@nasaprs.com.

• Meeting Location/Date

The HSR19 Week 1 Panels will be held at the St. Anthony Hotel, during January 7-10, 2020. Breakfast will be available between 7:00am-8:30am and Orientation will begin at 8:30am on Tuesday, January 7th.

• Hotel Accommodations
The St. Anthony Hotel is located at 300 East Travis Street, San Antonio, TX 78205. The hotel's phone number is (210) 237-47392. You do not need to call the hotel to make reservations, a confirmation number will be sent to you.

• Airline/Train Information

A new NASA policy requires that all business travel supported and paid by NRESS MUST be booked through our travel agent, Travel Leaders Corporate. NASA would appreciate you booking your flight as soon as possible as this will generate significant savings on airfare.

this will generate significant savings on airfare.

• Meal Arrangements and Refreshments
Breakfast, mid-morning break, hot lunch buffet and an afternoon break will be available each day.

The NRESS support team looks forward to working with you! this will generate significant savings on airfare.

❖ Sample Six Informing Buyer of Non-stock

Dear Ms. Lindsey,

Thank you for the order for 10 of our fish tanks that we recently received. The tanks are out of stock, as the order form you sent us is from our 2019 catalog which is no longer in use. I have enclosed our 2021 catalog and have marked the relevant pages for fish tanks. I would particularly recommend the Crystal series ranging from $400 to $1880 on page 62.

Delivery can be made within 14 working days.

We value your business and hope to be of service to you.

Yours sincerely,

Earl Thomas

Tasks to Fulfill

scan for the keys

1. Can you answer the questions?

(1) What is a good-news letter?
(2) What is a bad-news letter?
(3) What organizational patterns are recommended for good-news and neutral messages?
(4) What organizational patterns are recommended for bad-news messages?

2. Read and answer the following questions.

> Dear Mr. Lee,
>
> I am very much pleased to accept your offer regarding the deal we have previously been discussing.
>
> As we have agreed upon, we will be splitting the profits of this venture 50:50 and we will be meeting every Monday to discuss how this business venture is going along.
>
> I have enclosed a draft contract. Please return it after you have signed it.
>
> I look forward to working with you in this business.
>
> Sincerely yours,
>
> G. Zoe

Questions:

(1) Is it a good-news message or a bad-news message?
(2) How will the profit be split between the two parties?
(3) What will Mr. Lee and Mr. Zoe expect to do on Mondays concerning their business?
(4) What is enclosed in the letter?
(5) Which words in the letter have a similar meaning to the following?
　　A. proposal　　B. divide　　C. project

3. Fill in the blanks to complete the letter.

Dear Ms. Wells:

Certainly, you have a right to expect the best product and service from Burberry. And we do offer money-back guarantee to (1)_____ (确保我们顾客的满意).

What we can do in each instance is determined by (2)_____ (具体事实). With returned clothing, we generally (3)_____ (退款). Of course, to meet our obligation to our customers for quality merchandise, all (4)_____ (退回来的衣物) must be new. As the stains on your coat would prevent (5)_____ (无法再次销售), we must consider the sale final.

We appreciate your understanding and hope to meet your needs for years to come.

Regards,

Self-evaluation

1. Can you translate the following expressions into English?
(1) 好消息　　　(2) 坏消息　　　(3) 中性消息　　　(4) 缓冲　　　(5) 满足要求
(6) 拒绝要求　　(7) 维持良好关系　(8) 包装不好　　(9) 财政困难　(10) 经营成本

2. Please translate the sentences into English.
(1) 尽管我们尽可能地降低价格，但是从 6 月 15 日起，我们的价格将不得不提高 5%。
(2) 即使是价格做了调整，我们的产品价格依然是极具竞争力的。
(3) 我们完全理解您的困难，可是我们也要按时支付我们供货商的货款。
(4) 正是因为考虑到目前的经济形势，我们才同意您收到货物 60 天后付款。
(5) 大连供水集团将于 2021 年 4 月 11 日更换主管道，早 8 点至晚 6 点下列区域停水。
(6) 我们钦佩您为贫困儿童建立奖学金的努力。
(7) 对于您上周的工程招标，我们非常高兴提交我们的申报书和标书。
(8) 该公司服务佳，同行口碑好，在中国享有良好的声誉。
(9) 您上周订购 60 本《外贸英语入门》时，我们当时答应您立刻发货。
(10) 按您的要求，6 张松木梳妆台已于今天上午发出，预计 1 月初到达您处。
(11) 我们有与您想要的物品相似的货物，随函附上一张照片及其说明。

(12) 我们以最低的价格出售最好的产品为荣，而且我们保证不满意就退款，以确保您的满意。

(13) 谢谢您10月22日订购我们12件"帆"牌人衣，我们有现货，收到您的支票就立刻发货。

(14) 我们始终乐意帮助您这样的慈善机构。

(15) 很高兴告诉您，基金会批准了您的申请。

3. Please put the following sentences into Chinese.

(1) Congratulations! The Department of Atmospheric and Oceanic Science is pleased that you have been offered admission to the graduate program at UCLA.

(2) Thank you for your interest in graduate study at Colorado State University. You have been admitted to our Cognitive Psychology Program beginning with the fall semester of 2021.

(3) We only use the freshest blueberries and finest ingredients in our muffins and would be pleased to offer you a ten percent discount on this order.

(4) For the best interest of both of us, we will extend the credit when your current assets-to-liabilities ratio reaches 2 to 1.

(5) With the increase in requests we've received and because we are close to the end of a fiscal year, we have used all our travel funds for the year.

(6) As you know, the discount is allowed only when payment is made within ten days of billing.

(7) As Invoice No.226505 is now 45 days past this date, we are crediting your account with $945.07, leaving an unpaid balance of $29.23.

(8) Your March 29 order and accompanying request for credit were genuinely appreciated.

(9) As an individual's financial situation changes, we are always willing to reevaluate loan requests.

(10) Our review of your credit record requires that we serve you only on a cash basis at this time.

(11) While we are always willing and happy to assist researchers and students with their projects and assignments, some issues prevent us from approving your request.

(12) Thank you for your invitation to speak at the opening of the Graduate Students' Sports Events on April 28.

(13) I am pleased to tell you that we find the terms you have communicated to me in your previous letter acceptable.

(14) We are very happy to inform you that our November sales reached two million USD, 30% more than the forecasted figure.

(15) We are happy to announce a 50% discount on selected items from May 15 to 30 in all of our outlets to mark off the start of the holiday season.

4. Please polish the following letters.

(1)

Dear All,

As TEM 8 will be held in No.2 Teaching Building from 8am to 12am on Sunday, March 18, 2016, the building will be reserved for the examination.

Please be informed of this.

Teaching Office

(2)

Dear Ms. Freemont,

We regret to inform you that we cannot grant your request for a donation to the association's scholarship fund.

So many requests for contributions are made of us that we have found it necessary to budget a definite amount each year for this purpose. Our budgeted funds for this year have been exhausted, so we simply cannot consider additional requests. However, we will be able to consider your request next year.

We deeply regret our inability to help you now and trust that you understand our position.

Stephens

(3)

Dear Ms. Sanderson,

I regret to say that we must reject your request to replace Palm Vx organizer.

We must refuse because it is now past the 30-day return period. However we can repair it at your expenses if you like. Or you can buy another unit, which is $199 now, as we have recently dropped the price.

We trust that you will understand our position. We regret very much for the failure of the machine.

Yours,

Marilyn Cox,
Customer Relations

(4)

Dear Mr. Gates,

Thank you for thinking of us when you decided to open a charge account. Upon receiving your request, we looked into your credit history and found you have been quite intelligent in using credit in the past. We therefore are pleased to send you a Citi Bank credit card. The enclosed brochure describes many of the special services we offer our charge customers. As a charge customer, you may easily shop by telephone, and you will receive advance notification of sales.

We appreciate the opportunity to serve you, and we hope to merit your patronage for a long time.

Please remember that bills are mailed on the 20th of each month and are payable by the 15th of the next month. There is a finance of 1.5 percent on the unpaid balance each month.

Yours sincerely,

Bill Logan

(5)

Dear Mr. Chauvin

Your motor is no longer under warranty. We are not responsible for any products that are not under warranty.

From the photos and information you forwarded to us it can be concluded that your motor is more than four years old and it is no longer under warranty. We do however carry a wide variety of reasonably priced universal propellers, one of which I am sure will suit your needs.

Please call in at the store so we can help you get back out on the water soon.

Yours sincerely,

Stephen Clinton

(6)

Dear Mr. Long:

Thank you for your letter on May 7 concerning my outstanding account which is one week overdue.

According to my records and your letter on May 7, the outstanding balance is $3,500. I am not disputing this debt.

Before the enforced COVID-19 business closure, we had always been paid in full and on time. The mandatory shutdown of all non-essential businesses has led to temporary financial hardship for my business. Not being able to open my shop prohibits me from paying the amount you're demanding.

I've enclosed a check in the amount of $2500 as part payment on account as a show of good faith. I will try my best to remit the remaining $1000 within the next 30 days.
I apologize for not being able to make full payment on the due date.

Thank you for understanding.

Sincerely yours,

Kent Smith

Did you make any grammar mistake?
Did you make any spelling mistake?
Did you adopt the organizational patterns for good news, neutral and bad news respectively and correctly?

5. Can you write a letter with the details given in the box below, informing your supplier that an outstanding balance is being paid and explaining why the payment is late? Please pay attention to your organization of details.

> delay in payment, look into the matter, an oversight, US$ 20,000, being sent by telegraphic transfer, arrive within 24 hours, sorry for the inconvenience.

Did you put the main idea first?
Did you offer explanation for the delay?
Did you end the mail with a positive tone?

You can move on to Unit fifteen if you can complete the exercies satisfactorily.

Unit Fifteen

Miscellaneous Correspondence

"Miscellaneous" means "various types". Going by the meaning of this word, it can be said that miscellaneous correspondences are those that cover different subjects related to business. In other words, they are a collection of writings you employ in everyday business when coping with various matters, such as reservations, appointments, invitations, Thank You Letters, approvals, announcements, congratulations, sympathy etc.

Unit Objectives

After learning the unit, students should be able to:
1. Understand such business correspondence as invitations, replies to invitations, reservations, cancellation of reservations, thank you letters, congratulations;
2. Learn the appropriate expression, patterns and principles by heart;
3. Apply them in their business communications.

Structure & Content

Invitations

You write invitation letters when you want to invite people to a particular event or occasion, such as a business meeting, an opening ceremony or other events.

It is recommended that the writer extend the invitation right after addressing the recipient of the letter, then go on to the relevant details about the time, venue, and date of the event. In the letter, you should provide contact address where the recipient can reach you, and you may also request a feedback, e.g. confirmation of attendance. It is common that the invitation is extended again in the end of the letter.

❖ Sample One Inviting a Speaker to Talk at a Conference

Dear Prof. Carol Allen,

It is with great pleasure that I invite you to present a 25-minute talk at the 19th Annual International Marketing Conference to be held at the La Posada de Santa Fe Hotel, Santa Fe, New Mexico, USA from March 9 - 13, 2022 (Welcome reception and evening registration begins on Sunday, March 8). — *Extending the invitation revealing the time and place of the event*

The theme of the meeting will be "Davos Man & Manila Woman: Globalization at Crossroad" and will follow the same format as before with 25-minute presentations punctuated by selected 40-minute invited talks that will explore various themes in greater detail. — *Revealing the theme*

Information regarding registration, abstract submission, and accommodation deadlines can be found on the conference website: https://www.davomeetings.com/conference/22thannual/index.html — *Listing the details for next action*

Dear Prof. Allen, we hope that you will be able to join us for a meeting that will be of great interest and topicality. We look forward to seeing you in Santa Fe, New Mexico. — *Extending invitation again*

All the best,

Prof. Zonk

❖ Sample Two Inviting a Scholar to Review a Paper

Dear Dr. Zou,

In recognition of your expertise in this field, I am writing to ask you to review, 2021JA028730: "Mobile Payment and Financial Security" by Hill et al., which has been submitted to Journal of International Business. Full author details and abstract are below.

Extending the invitation

Please note, we request review comments within 21 days of your acceptance.

Listing specific request

Please let us know your decision as soon as possible. This will help us provide our authors with a timely and efficient review process.

Asking for an immediate feedback

Thank you very much for your support of Journal of International Business.

Expressing appreciation

Sincerely,
Journal of International Business

❖ Sample Three Inviting a Distinguished Guest to a Sports Event

Dear Mr. Zhang,

As one of our distinguished guests, you are invited to be the guest of the 32nd Sports Meeting for Postgraduates to be held in the school stadium at 8:30 a.m. on May 20th. — *Extending invitation*

The purpose of this meeting is to popularize sports and enhance constitution of young students, which remains a popular campus tradition for more than 30 years. — *Mentioning theme of the event*

We hope you will be able to accept this invitation. And we would appreciate it if you could inform us of your decision before May 10th, 2021. — *Calling for immediate action*

Sincerely,

Lucy Max

Replies

If your reply to an invitation is "yes", you will say so in the beginning and express your gratitude for the invitation. You then proceed to tell the receiver what you intend to do next before closing the letter by showing gratitude again or saying you are looking forward to the event/meeting the receiver of the letter.

❖ Sample Four Accepting Invitations

Dear Mr. Zonk:

Subject: Accepting the invitation to speak at the 19th Annual International Marketing Conference

I feel honored to be given the opportunity to deliver a 25-minute talk at the 19th Annual International Marketing Conference, and it is with greatly pleasure that I accept your kind proposal.

Accepting the invitation and expressing gratitude

I have already started to make my travel arrangements to the venue, and I will arrive at least a day before the conference.

Telling the reader your future plan

Thanks a lot for inviting me to speak at the conference.

Expressing gratitude for the invitation

Thank You,
Yours Truly

Kim Biden

❖ Sample Five Accepting an Invitation

Dear Miss Harris,

Your invitation for me to act as the chairperson for the 15th upcoming Space and Ocean Conference is an honor. I shall be very happy to be part of the event hosted by your organization.

I enjoyed serving in that role last year. Your committee members are an excellent group with great ideas, and it was a privilege to work with them.

I shall make my own travel arrangement and be there one day before the start of the conference.

I look forward to seeing you soon.

Yours,

M. Allen

Accepting the invitation and expressing appreciation

Showing good memory of the past cooperation

Revealing future action

Expressing positive attitude

❖ Sample Six Declining an Invitation

If you have to say "no" to an invitation, it's important that you express your gratitude toward the invitation before declining the offer. A reason for the "no" should be provided. The letter should be closed with a positive tone.

Dear Ms. Young:

I appreciate your dinner invitation for February 9. I have always enjoyed my time spent with your loving family.

Appreciating the offer

Unfortunately, I will be out of town on business from February 7 to 14 for trip in Shanghai.

Saying "no" and offering reasons

I wish you can extend similar invitations in the future.

Friendly inviting further communication

Thank you for your kind invitation.

Positive close

Yours,

Kim

Reservations

People make reservations for various purposes, such as to ensure that they can get a room in a hotel, a table in a restaurant, or a seat on an airplane. Such correspondences are concise and direct. Writers tend to go to the main point in the very beginning and follow it up with secondary details.

❖ Sample Seven Reserving a Hotel Room

Dear Sir or Madam,	
Please reserve a double room with single occupancy of executive class from 25th to 28th May. Mr. Yuan Fan, our Managing Director, will be staying in the city and he will be checking in around 10.00 am on 25th May.	*Making the reservation*
We would like you to confirm this booking within 24 hours.	*Asking for confirmation of booking*
You may kindly forward the bills to us directly for settlement. As in the past, we will send the check within 3 days after receipt of your bills. Please allow 10% discount on the room rent as per our agreement.	*Details about methods of payment*
Thank you. Faithfully *James Felony*	*Friendly close*

❖ Sample Eight Reserving a Hotel Room with Special Requirements

Dear Sir or Madam,

I would like to reserve a double room for five nights from June the 4th to 8th inclusive. My husband is confined to a wheelchair, so we need to have a shower stall and a room which are wheelchair accessible. Please note that we will be arriving around 5:00 p.m. on June 4th.

I am enclosing a check for $100.00 as a deposit. Please send written confirmation of this reservation to me at the above address. If you have any questions, my phone number is 310-5705.

We are looking forward to our stay at Furama Hotel, Dalian. Thank you very much.

Faithfully,

Luna Alexander

Making the reservation making specific requirements

Mentioning a deposit check is enclosed

A positive close

❖ Sample Nine Reserving a Cruise

Dear Mr. Floyd,

As per our phone conversation of May 5, enclosed is a money order for ￥2000.00. This amount guarantees my reservation for two adults aboard your South Sea Spectacular Cruise leaving Guangzhou on May 24, and returning June 4, 2020.

The total cost for this trip is ￥8,000.00, and I understand that the balance of ￥6000.00 will be paid by May 24.

I understand also that my ￥2000.00 deposit is refundable in full if you receive a written request of cancellation no later than May 10.

Yours sincerely,

Clair Dai

Making reservation

Mentioning a money order is enclosed

Mentioning the remaining will be paid later
Stressing the deposit is refundable

❖ Sample Ten Cancelling a Reservation

Dear Mr. Robinson,	
My organization was planning to use your banquet hall for the annual awards dinner on Thursday, December 24. We have just been informed, however, that the event will have to be suspended until further notice on account of weather. We therefore are forced to cancel the reservation.	*Original plan to be cancelled* *Reasons for the decision*
Thank you for all the trouble you went through to make the arrangements. We will certainly keep your agency in mind for similar purposes in the future.	*Positive close*
Yours,	
M. Baker	

Confirmation is needed when the writer wants to make sure of a registration made or a business proposal concluded

❖ Sample Eleven Confirming a Registration

Dear Miss Ma,	
This letter is to confirm my registration at the Davos annual convention on July 25, 2019. Enclosed you will find a check for $250.00, as is requested of me.	*Confirming registration*
May I remind you that I have yet to receive my information packet? As the day of the convention is rapidly approaching, could you please express mail the packet and confirmation of my registration to the address above?	*Making request*
I appreciate your help and look forward to attending the convention.	*Positive close*
Yours,	
Luna Lee	

Appointments

When we plan to meet with someone for official discussions, we set a date and time to meet or see them, thus making an appointment. It is vital that clear and complete details be given.

❖ Sample Twelve Asking for an Appointment

Dear Olof,	
I was wondering if we could have a talk about the installation at your factory.	*Asking for an appointment*
I shall be glad if we can meet in your office around 10am on September 15, 2021. Please kindly let me know if you will be available then, or the time that suits you for us to meet in person.	*Details*
I look forward to hearing from you soon.	*Inviting feedback*
Sincerely yours,	
Helen	

❖ Sample Thirteen Confirming an Appointment

Dear Natalia,

This is to confirm my travel plans to Boston and to thank you for offering to meet me at the airport and drive me to my hotel.

I will be arriving at the Logan International Airport on August 8, at 11:50 a.m. on China Southern Airlines, flight 697. Please meet me at the arrival gate.

I look forward to seeing you soon.

Yours sincerely,

Issae Biden

— Confirming the appointment

— Confirming details

— Positive close

❖ Sample Fourteen Canceling an Appointment

When we have to change or cancel an appointment made, we should inform the people involved. An explanation is expected for the cancellation.

Dear Mr. Bush,

I am sorry that I must cancel my appointment to see the Governor at noon on December 21. My mother has been hospitalized for heart surgery and it is important that I be with her at this time. I anticipate that I will be in Boston for the next month.

The most important detail first
Reasons for the decision

Before I return home, I will contact your office to reschedule my appointment. Please send the information I requested to my home address. My mail will be forwarded to me in Boston.

Follow-up plan

I apologize for the inconvenience and appreciate your understanding.

Apologizing and expressing appreciation

Sincerely yours,

Kate Larry

❖ Sample Fifteen Apologizing for Missing an Appointment

When we unfortunately miss an appointment, we should apologize.

Dear Kim,

I am sorry I missed our appointment yesterday. Ever since we agreed to meet for detailed discussion on the plan, I had been looking forward to it. But when I rechecked my calendar today, I discovered that the meeting was actually scheduled for yesterday.

I realize how busy you are and that your time is valuable, but I hope this oversight will not prevent us from rescheduling our appointment. Meeting with you means a great deal to me, and I assure you, this will not happen again.

Please forgive my absent-mindedness. I am looking forward to hearing from you soon.

Yours,

James Cameron

Apologizing first

Explanations

Showing appreciation of the partner's time and effort
Asking for a new appointment

Positive close

Congratulations

It is customary that you write a congratulation letter to praise someone for their achievement and success. The message should be sent immediately and it should be positive, simple, and straight to the point.

In the letter, you should first tell the purpose of the letter, and proceed to praise the exact achievement he/she has made.

❖ Sample Sixteen Congratulation Letters on Promotion

Letter	Annotation
Dear B. Brown,	
I would like to sincerely congratulate you on your recent promotion.	*Congratulation first*
I must say that you deserve the promotion. I have noted how smart and hardworking you have been over the past years. It is obvious that you have a bright future ahead of you. I am sure that you will achieve more with your gifts and dedications.	*Complimentary*
I wish you all the best in your future career and life endeavors.	*Goodwill*
Yours sincerely,	
Bruice Stone	

❖ Sample Seventeen Congratulating on Award

Dear Dr. Liang,

As President of the AGU Space Physics Section, it is my pleasure to congratulate you on winning an Outstanding Student Paper Award for your presentation at the 2019 AGU Fall Meeting in San Francisco. Your paper, entitled "Impact of Heavy Ions on Reconnection Rate and Dipolarization Fronts during Magnetotail reconnection," was one of the 10 winners in the Space Physics Section. This award is a significant recognition and you should be very proud. Motivated youth scientists like you are crucial to the future success of our discipline.

Purpose of writing the letter
Stating the award --- the most important message

We are enclosing a certificate that formally acknowledges your accomplishments. In addition, you will receive a complimentary ticket to the SPA banquet in San Francisco this coming December, where we will introduce the OSPA winners. Finally, you and the other winners will be listed in Eos.

Discussing the significance of the achievement. Informing more details

Congratulations again! I look forward to seeing you at future AGU meetings and following the progress of your research.

Sincerely,

David G. Sibeck

Congratulating again and Kindly encouraging future progress

❖ Sample Eighteen Congratulating on Bonus Payout

Dear Monika,

Congratulations!

I am pleased to tell you that your rating for the quarter ending was Rank One, the payout due to you being ￥60000. The details are attached for your reference to enable you to understand the calculations. And you are most welcome to contact the HR department to seek for any clarifications.

We hope to see more of such ratings from you and wish you all the best for all your efforts with us.

With regards,

Tom Cameron

Good news first

Details of the good news

Encouragement and goodwill

Thank-You Letters

It is always important to show our appreciation to the people who have helped us. A well written appreciation letter can improve relationships and can also open doors for further opportunities. There are different types of appreciation letters, such as business appreciation letter, employee appreciation letter, staff appreciation letter, teacher appreciation letter etc.

When writing Thank You letters, you should specify why you appreciate the receiver of the letter and your desire to reciprocate him/her if you intend to do so.

❖ Sample Nineteen Thank-you Letter

Dear Ms. Scott,	
Let me send my sincere thanks for the wonderful time I spent at your plant last week.	*Expressing gratitude first*
Arrangements for workshop tour and office meetings were wonderful. I wish I could stay longer.	*Specifying the appreciation*
I will always remember the happy and fruitful week I spent with you and in the company of your team.	*Restating the hospitality received*
I hope you will visit us soon so that I can reciprocate your kindness.	*Intending to reciprocate*
Best regards,	
W. Nelson	

Tasks to Fulfill

scan for the keys

1. Can you answer the questions?

(1) What does "miscellaneous" mean?

(2) If you are going to invite someone to a meeting, how would you like to compose the letter?

(3) When you are making a reservation, what sort of details will you include?

(4) Should you praise the specific achievement when you congratulate a person?

2. Please read the letter and answer the questions.

> Dear Kim,
>
> I am sorry I missed our appointment yesterday. Ever since we agreed to meet for detailed discussion on the plan, I had been looking forward to it. But when I rechecked my calendar today, I discovered that the meeting was actually scheduled for yesterday.
>
> I realize how busy you are and that your time is valuable, and I am terribly sorry for this oversight. I assure you this will not happen again.
>
> Will you please kindly let me know the time that suits you for us to reschedule our appointment? Meeting with you means a great deal to me.
>
> I am looking forward to hearing from you soon.
>
> Yours,
>
> *Eliza Bungan*

Questions:

(1) Why did Eliza Bungan apologize?

(2) How did she miss it?

(3) How did Eliza ask for a new appointment?

(4) Does she believe it is important for them to meet?

(5) Which words in the letter have a similar meaning to the following?

   A. look into again   B. agenda   C. arranged   D. negligence

3. Please fill in the blanks to complete the letter.

I am sorry that I must (1)_____ （取消约会） to see the Governor at noon on December 21. My mother had a heart attack and is (2)_____ （住院） for heart surgery. It is important that I (3)_____ （陪伴她） at this time. I anticipate that I will be in Boston for the next month.

Before I return home, I will contact your office to (4)_____ （重新定时间会面）. Please send the information I requested to my home address. My mail will be forwarded to me in Boston.

I apologize for the inconveniences and (5)_____ （感谢您的理解）.

Self-evaluation

1. Can you translate the following expressions into English.

(1) 日程　　　(2) 安排约会　　(3) 取消预约　　(4) 错过约会　　(5) 按时赴约
(6) 预订宾馆　(7) 预订餐席　　(8) 取消预订　　(9) 定金　　　　(10) 预订机票
(11) 邀请参加　(12) 接受邀请　 (13) 拒绝邀请　(14) 邀请评审　　(15) 感谢邀请
(16) 感谢信　　(17) 祝贺升职　 (18) 诚挚祝贺　(19) 感谢款待　　(20) 回报

2. Please translate the sentences into English.

(1) 您在业界享有名望，我们很高兴请您当会议的主席。
(2) 如果能接受我们的邀请来当会议的嘉宾，我们不胜感激。
(3) 很荣幸接受您的邀请。
(4) 今年我将参加希腊的一个展会。希望下次能得到您的邀请。
(5) 谢谢您邀请我参加你们的开幕典礼。我将准时到场。
(6) 请为我预订 2 个双人间，从 10 月 12 日到 14 日，共计 3 天。
(7) 我们需要您预交 300 元的定金。
(8) 对不起，因为天气原因，预订的酒席需取消。
(9) 目前机票比较紧张，请尽快预订。
(10) 对不起，预订满了。
(11) 下周您有时间吗？我想和您约个时间谈谈。
(12) 对不起，我不得不取消咱们的约会，我母亲摔断了腿要手术。
(13) 布朗先生把约会全忘掉了。他非常抱歉。
(14) 我是否可以把和您的约会从周一改至周三？

(15) 祝贺您！很高兴通知您，您的申请得到了国家自然科学基金 $400,000 美金的资助。

3. Please put the following sentences into Chinese.
(1) It is with great pleasure that I invite you to present a 10-minute talk at the 19th Annual International Marketing Conference.
(2) The meeting will be held in Beijing Friendship Hotel, from March 9 - 13, 2022 (Welcome Reception and evening registration begins Sunday, March 8).
(3) In recognition of your expertise in this field, I am writing to ask you to participate in a committee organized by ministry of Commerce.
(4) I feel honored to be given the opportunity to take part in the conference.
(5) It is with great pleasure that I accept your kind invitation.
(6) Please let us know your decision as soon as possible.
(7) Please reserve a double room with single occupancy of executive class for 4 nights, from June 3-6, inclusive.
(8) Please send written confirmation of this reservation to me within 48 hours.
(9) I am sorry that we have to cancel the reservation on account of extreme weather.
(10) I will be travelling to Tokyo on flight CA658 next Monday morning. Please meet me at the arrival gate of Airport Japan at 10:05 am, 1 August.
(11) I am sorry I missed our appointment, and I will contact your office to reschedule an appointment.
(12) When I rechecked my calendar today, I discovered that the meeting was actually scheduled for yesterday.
(13) I realize how busy you are and that your time is valuable, but I hope this oversight will not prevent us from rescheduling our appointment.
(14) I wish you all the best in your future career and life endeavors.
(15) I will always remember the wonderful time I spent with you and in the company of your team.

4. Please write appropriate business correspondences according to the information below.
(1) Please write a letter inviting important customers to participate an event organized by your company.
(2) Please write to book a hotel room for your boss who will travel to New York on business
(3) You are writing an email, cancelling an appointment.
(4) One of your employees has won a first prize in a contest, and you are writing a letter of

congratulation to him/her.

(5) You are invited to speak on "Space and Survival" in a local high school but you just cannot make it. Write to decline the offer.

Did you make any grammar mistake?
Did you make any spelling mistake?
Did you apply the correct business words and adopt proper patterns in your sentences?
Did you arrange the details of the message in the appropriate order?

Congratulations to you all! I wish you more progress and bigger success!